UML™ Softw with Visual Studio® 2010

What you need to know, and no more!

Tony Loton

LOTON *tech*

www.lotontech.com

Copyright © Tony Loton / LOTONtech Limited 2010.

This edition published by LOTONtech Limited (www.lotontech.com).

ISBN-13: 9781440490859

ISBN-10: 1440490856

All rights reserved. No part of this publication may be reproduced or distributed in any form or by any means without the prior permission of the author and / or publisher.

The material in this book is provided for educational purposes only. No responsibility for loss occasioned to any person or corporate body acting or refraining to act as a result of reading material in this book can be accepted by the author or publisher.

All trademarks are the property of their respective owners. LOTONtech Limited is not associated with any product or vendor mentioned in this book except where stated.

Unless otherwise stated; any third-party quotes, images and screenshots, or portions thereof, are included under 'fair use' for comment, news reporting, teaching, scholarship, and research.

Contents

About the Author	9
About this Book	11
BOOK POSITIONING	11
TERMINOLOGY	13
Acknowledgements	14
1 – UML, End-to-End	15
WHAT IS UML, AND WHY SHOULD YOU USE IT?	15
UML vs. DSL	17
A BRIEF HISTORY OF UML	17
UML DIAGRAMS AND THEIR RELATIONSHIPS	18
SUMMARY	21
2 – A Brief History of UML with Visual Studio	23
VISIO FOR ENTERPRISE ARCHITECTS	23
DOMAIN SPECIFIC LANGUAGES	24
VISUAL STUDIO 2010 ULTIMATE EDITION	24
SUMMARY	25
3 – Visual Studio 2010 UML for Analysts and Designers	27
VISUAL STUDIO 2010 MODELING PROJECT	27

A NOTE ABOUT UML MODELS AND DIAGRAMS	28
UML USE CASE DIAGRAM	29
Example Use Case Diagram	31
About Use Case Specifications	34
UML SEQUENCE DIAGRAM	35
UML Model Explorer and the Toolbox	35
Creating the Sequence Diagram, Step-by-Step	37
Sequence Diagram Additional Notes	41
UML CLASS DIAGRAM	44
UML ACTIVITY DIAGRAM	51
About State-Chart Diagrams	56
UML COMPONENT DIAGRAM	58
WHAT'S MISSING IN VISUAL STUDIO 2010 UML?	61
FROM UML TO CODE	62
SUMMARY	62
4 – Best Practices and the Software Development Process	**63**
HOW TO COPY AND PASTE UML DIAGRAMS	63
UML NOTATION STYLE GUIDELINES	64
UML PROFILES AND STEREOTYPES	65
STRUCTURING THE MODEL	67

MODELING AND VALIDATING THE ARCHITECTURE	69
Architecture Explorer	70
SOFTWARE DEVELOPMENT PROCESSES	70
Actors and Use Cases vs. Personas and Scenarios	71
Microsoft Team Foundation Server	72
TOP-DOWN, BOTTOM-UP, AND ITERATIVE MODELING	73
SUMMARY	74

5 – Visual Studio 2010 UML for Developers — 75

CLASS DESIGNER	75
REVERSE ENGINEERING SEQUENCE DIAGRAMS	81
How to Reverse Engineer a Sequence Diagram	81
Reverse Engineering in Visual Studio 2010	83
CREATING LAYER DIAGRAMS	86
Validating the Architecture	88
DEPENDENCY GRAPHS / DIRECTED GRAPH DOCUMENTS	90
Analyzing Dependencies	91
ARCHITECTURE EXPLORER	92
SUMMARY	94

6 – Visualization and Modeling Feature Pack — 95

CODE GENERATION AND REVERSE ENGINEERING	95

XMI Import	96
Exploring C and C++ Code in Architecture Explorer	97
Summary	97
7 – Visio 2010 UML	**99**
Top-Down Software Design	100
Code Generation	100
Reverse Engineering	100
Reverse Engineering into Visio 2010	*101*
Reverse Engineering, No Source Code Required	*103*
Summary	105
Appendix A – RE.NET Reverse Engineering C# Code	**107**
Step 1 – Create Visual Studio Project	107
Step 2 – Build and Locate the Executable File	107
Step 3 – Run the Utility	107
Step 4 – Add Results to a new Class Library Project	108
Step 5 – Reverse Engineer the Source Code Class Stubs	108
ReverseEngineer.cs Reverse Engineering Source Code	108
Appendix B – Visual Modeling Web Site	**117**
Glossary of Acronyms	**119**
Also by Tony Loton	**121**

Table of Figures	**123**
Index	**127**

About the Author

Tony Loton has been a Microsoft Certified Professional (MCP) since 2004. He is a Microsoft Solutions Framework (MSF) Practitioner, and he has held the position of 'Head of Microsoft Practice' at two UK consultancy companies that enjoyed Microsoft Gold Certified Partner status.

Tony has a long history of working with, and teaching, the Unified Modeling Language (UML) and associated software development processes including the Rational Unified Process (RUP) and Microsoft Solutions Framework (MSF).

In 2005, Tony Loton co-authored the book 'Professional Visual Studio 2005 Team System' for Wrox Press, in which he contributed chapters on the Visual Studio software design tools: Application Designer, Logical Datacenter Designer, System Designer, and the UML-like Class Designer. He was also commissioned by Microsoft to write a series of articles on these software design tools for the on-line Microsoft Developer Network (MSDN) developer center.

Earlier in 2002, Tony co-authored the book 'Professional UML with Visual Studio .NET' for Wrox Press. The book you are reading now might be thought of as a natural – if somewhat belated – successor to that book.

UML Software Design with Visual Studio 2010

About this Book

The purpose of this book is to provide a fairly gentle coverage of the new Unified Modeling Language (UML) features of Visual Studio 2010. Whether you are encountering UML for the first time or migrating from another UML tool and programming environment, let's say Enterprise Architect + Java, you should find something of interest in this book. And, if you have read the earlier book that I co-authored ("Professional UML with Visual Studio .NET"), you may regard this book as a natural successor.

To gain maximum advantage from this book you will need the *Visual Studio 2010 Ultimate Edition* that allows you to create the UML diagrams discussed herein. Users of the *Visual Studio 2010 Premium Edition* can access the same diagrams in read-only fashion, so an understanding of these diagrams may be beneficial to you too. There is also something in here for users of the *Visual Studio 2010 Professional + Visio 2010 Professional* combo; so you might benefit from the generic UML coverage herein irrespective of your development tools set-up.

Book Positioning

This book covers the intersection of Visual Studio 2010 and UML, and to some extent Visio 2010, as indicated by the **THIS BOOK** label in *Figure 1 Positioning of This Book*.

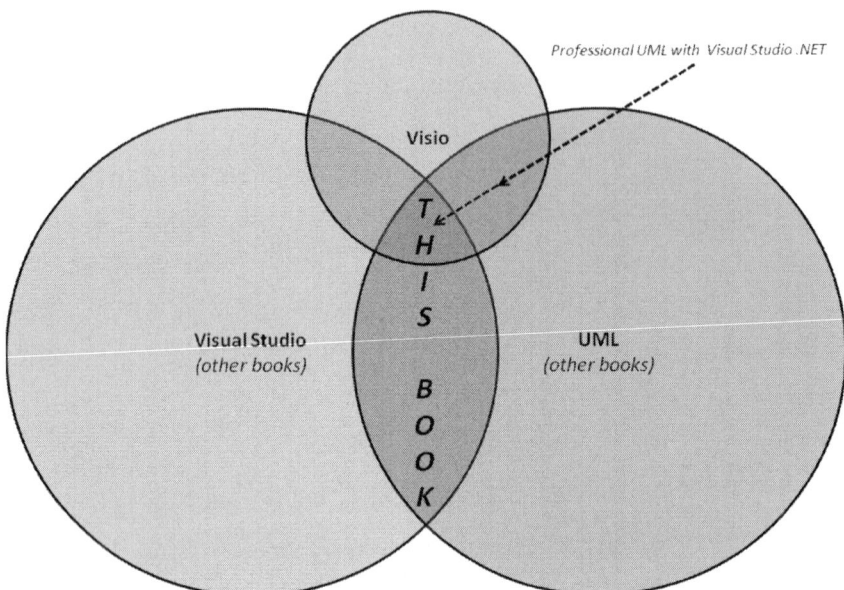

Figure 1 Positioning of This Book

It is not my intention to provide a complete coverage of all the nuts and bolts of UML, which you will find documented in many other good books. Nor is my intention to provide a comprehensive guide to the full Visual Studio 2010 IDE feature set where those features do not relate to UML.

I will not repeat verbatim the information given in my earlier book that focused on the interplay between Visual Studio .NET and Visio for Enterprise Architects. *Chapter 7 – Visio 2010 UML* tells you why this legacy approach may still be relevant, and the original book is still in print.

While this book is timed to coincide with the at-the-time-of-writing latest Visual Studio 2010, I expect it to remain current for some time even as future versions of Visual Studio are released. New software versions tend to offer cumulative functionality to the extent that – for example – some of the guidance provided in books about Microsoft

Word 2003 may still be useful to users of the latest Microsoft Office 2010.

Terminology

Various strands of history have converged to form the Visual Studio 2010 UML offering: different software development languages, open source vs. proprietary development, UML-compliant and DSL-specific notations, and so on. Add into the mix my own history originally as a Java developer / architect and UML practitioner, then as a Microsoft .NET developer / architect and MSF practitioner, and we have a recipe for mixed terminology.

Throughout this book you will necessarily encounter different terms used for essentially the same concepts; for example the functions that an object performs are sometimes referred to as *methods* and sometimes as *operations*. Depending on the origin of my examples you will sometimes see an object's *methods* (or *operations*) written in PascalCase (each word capitalized) and sometimes in camelCase (the second and subsequent words capitalized). It's the same for an object's *fields*... or *attributes*.

I make little apology for this for the simple reason that as you read other books about object oriented software development, UML, .NET, and other associated techniques and technologies, you will in any case encounter these various terminologies; and you'll have to get used to making the mental translations between similar terms.

Due to its technical nature, this book is peppered with acronyms. While each one should be spelled out on first usage, and periodically thereafter, you will no doubt benefit from the handy *Glossary* that I have included at the end of the book.

Tony Loton

Acknowledgements

This book has predominantly been a sole endeavor. I knew what I wanted to say, and how I wanted to say it. Most importantly, I wanted to say it while it was still at its most relevant in this fast-moving world of software development. In this context I judged that a long-drawn-out collaborative book writing project would have been detrimental.

In a sense, though, I *have* collaborated... because this book builds on some of the ideas first developed in my co-authored books *Professional UML with Visual Studio .NET* and *Professional Visual Studio 2005 Team System*. If I hadn't worked on those books, I would not have written this one. So I'd like to thank my co-authors of those books for their indirect assistance.

On the same basis, I should give thanks indirectly to Grady Booch, Ivar Jacobson and Jim Rumbaugh, without whom there would be no UML to write about.

I'll stop short of thanking my parents, without whom there would be no author to write this book, but I will extend thanks to my wife Debbie – my ever-vigilant (and sometimes too vigilant!) proof-reader.

The occasional *UML Style Tips* peppered throughout the book take inspiration from Scott Ambler's book "Elements of UML Style" published by Cambridge Press, which I heartily recommend.

1 – UML, End-to-End

The purpose of this chapter is to set the scene by reviewing the key UML concepts and diagram types, the important – and often overlooked – relationships between these diagrams, and the role of UML in the software development process. For UML virgins this will serve as a practical introduction that will help you make sense of the rest of the book; and for UML practitioners it will serve as handy revision.

What is UML, and Why Should You Use It?

Here I expand on the original definition of the Unified Modeling Language that was included in my earlier UML book:

*The **Unified Modeling Language** is a **notation**; a set of diagrams and diagram elements that may be arranged to describe the analysis of a business problem or the design of a software solution. **UML** is not a **software development process**, nor is it a **method** comprising a notation and a process.*

In theory you can apply aspects of the notation according to the steps prescribed by any software development process you choose – traditional waterfall, extreme programming, Rapid Application Development (RAD) or Agile – but in practice you will probably adhere to the Microsoft Solutions Framework (MSF) process enacted by the Team Foundation Server (TFS).

Now that you know what UML is, you might still wonder why you need an object oriented software modeling notation. The classic argument goes like this:

- To build a bridge across a small stream you could simply lay a plank of wood from one side to the other, and you could do so on your own. If it didn't hold up, the worst case outcome would be wet feet.

- To build a bridge across a narrow river you would need to do some forward thinking (i.e. estimation) about the materials you need – wood, brick, or metal – and how much of each. You would need some help, and your helpers would need to know what kind of bridge you're trying to build.

- To build a bridge across a very wide river you would need to do even more planning, and you'd be communicating with a much bigger team. For this commercial-scale development you would need to liaise with the planning authorities and would have to comply with any health-and-safety regulations. You would also need to lodge sufficient legacy documentation for the structure to be maintained far into the future.

In other words: the bigger and more complex the project, and the more people involved, the more important it is to undertake a formal design exercise. And this applies to software projects too where it is necessary to:

- Establish a blueprint for the software solution.

- Estimate and plan the time and materials.

- Communicate within the team, and across teams.

- Document the project.

Don't discount the final bullet point: using UML merely to document a project. More projects than I care to mention have benefitted from documenting a project in UML retrospectively when little or no up-front design has been undertaken. Someone – who may be a different developer or an entirely different overseas team – will have to maintain the software in the future, long after the original team has disbanded or the original developer has left the company. They will benefit from having more than just the code to describe the system.

UML vs. DSL

With Microsoft having flitted between the Unified Modeling Language (UML) and Domain Specific Languages (DSL, see next chapter), one might be left wondering whether it is worth using UML instead of, or as well as, a DSL.

From a practical perspective, UML has for some time been an *industry standard* visual modeling notation. There's a good chance of finding other people who understand it, and a good chance of finding training courses and books (like this one) that show you how to use it.

A Brief History of UML

The Unified Modeling Language (UML) is a modeling language, obviously. But what makes it unified?

Prior to unification the plethora of object oriented 'methods' included the *Booch Method* devised by Grady Booch, the *Object Modeling Technique* devised by Jim Rumbaugh, and *Object Oriented Software Engineering* (also known as *Objectory*) devised by Ivar Jacobson.

These 'methods' expressed essentially the same ideas, but using different notations, and each focused on a different aspect of software development; for example Jacobson introduced the idea of use cases to describe user requirements whereas the other methods did not have any direct equivalent.

Tony Loton

The unification of these three methods began in 1994 and concluded with UML version 1.1 being adopted by the Object Management Group (OMG) in 1997. The OMG, which is an industry consortium now including Microsoft, has been the custodian of the UML specification ever since.

If you speak to anyone who claims to be doing *object modeling*, the chances are they'll be conversant with UML.

UML Diagrams and Their Relationships

Visual Studio 2010 supports the five UML diagrams listed below; which at the time of writing excludes UML *collaboration diagrams* and *state-chart diagrams*.

Activity Diagram: resembles a traditional flowchart and is typically used to model a business process comprising a number of use cases, or the flow of activities within a specific use case, or the logic of a business rule.

Use Case Diagram: shows which people or other systems (the 'actors') will use which functions provided by the software solution; i.e. it models the user requirements.

Sequence Diagram: realizes a use case by showing how objects interact in sequence in order to provide the functionality described by the use case.

Class Diagram: shows how object classes in the software solution relate to each other in terms of their static relationships; in the context of a specific use case (the 'participating classes') or on a package-by-package basis.

Component Diagram: is an architecture-level artifact that shows the relationship between deployable components (such as DLLs and EXEs) that contain classes.

Many of the books and training courses that I have encountered over the years treat each of these diagrams in isolation; so readers and attendees have a good comprehension of where each diagram may be useful but not how the artifacts in the various diagrams *might relate to each other*. I hope to put this right with my *Figure 2 End-to-End UML*. Don't worry, you don't need to read the minute details within each diagram; just take note of my comments about how they interrelate.

When used to model an overarching business process, the activities defined in an *Activity Diagram* might be reflected as use cases in the *Use Case Diagram*. So, for an activity-diagram action named Pick Stock, you might expect there to be a corresponding use case of the same name – otherwise, you might doubt the integrity of the solution.

Each use case defined on a *Use Case Diagram* (there may be more than one such diagram) would be *realized* in the form of a *Sequence Diagram*. If you find a sequence diagram without a corresponding use case, or vice versa, you might doubt the integrity of the solution.

For each use case there may also be a corresponding 'Participating Classes' *Class Diagram*, showing the static relationships between the classes that interact in the use case realization *Sequence Diagram*. Where an inter-object message on the sequence diagram does not have a corresponding *operation* on the recipient class in the participating classes diagram (*Class Diagram*) you might doubt the integrity of the solution.

Classes will be packaged into components (such as .NET assembly DLLs) for deployment, and these components could – but don't have to – reflect the division of use cases into *subsystems* on the *Use Case Diagram*.

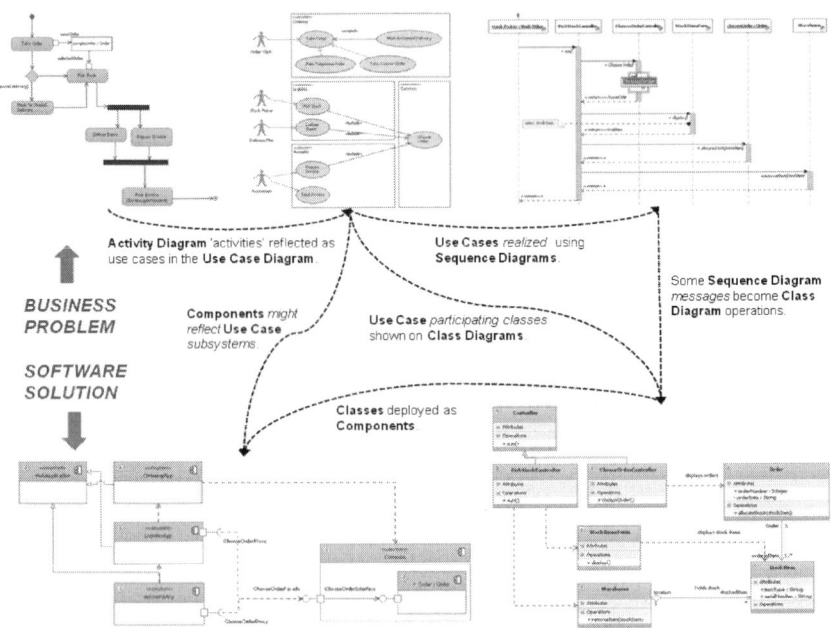

Figure 2 End-to-End UML

Don't take my foregoing narrative literally. For example: you don't have to use activity diagrams to model the flow between individual use cases, but it might help to assure complete coverage if you do so; and you don't have to devise deployable components that mirror use case subsystems, but it is one possible scheme. My objective here is merely to encourage you to think about the possible relationships between diagrams, and how one diagram might be used to cross-reference another diagram, rather than thinking about each diagram type entirely in isolation.

That's what I mean by end-to-end UML.

Summary

In this chapter you have learnt why visual modeling with UML is important, how UML originated, and how the various UML diagrams relate to one another.

UML Software Design with Visual Studio 2010

2 – A Brief History of UML with Visual Studio

Microsoft seems to have had something of an on-off relationship with the Unified Modeling Language (UML) since its creation out of three precursor visual modeling methods in the mid-1990s. In a world dominated originally by Rational Software Corporation and its Rational Rose (later Rational XDE) UML modeling tool, and with a supporting cast of alternative UML tool vendors, Microsoft was somewhat conspicuous by its absence.

Visio for Enterprise Architects

To coincide with the Visual Studio .NET Integrated Development Environment (IDE) around 2003, Microsoft upgraded its popular Visio diagram-creation product to full 'Visio for Enterprise Architects' status. This tool provided not only a UML drawing feature, but also the important abilities to generate .NET code stubs from a UML model and to reverse engineer a UML model from a .NET software solution. It satisfied the minimum requirement for a UML modeling tool, but lagged the capabilities of the dedicated tools from other vendors. Rational XDE, in particular, provided good integration of UML into the Visual Studio IDE itself.

Visio for Enterprise Architects was documented in my earlier co-authored book 'Professional UML with Visual Studio .NET : Unmasking Visio for Enterprise Architects'.

Tony Loton

Domain Specific Languages

With the introduction of the Team System variants of Visual Studio in 2005, Microsoft appeared to move in on another market dominated by Rational Software Corporation – that of software development process enactment – yet at the same time appeared to change tack on formal support for UML. The bright new thing coming out of Microsoft at the time was the Doman Specific Language (DSL) approach to devising modeling languages finely tuned for specific software modeling tasks, as an alternative to the general purpose UML approach to Model Driven Architecture (MDA). The first DSLs to be included in Visual Studio were the *Application Designer* (which resembled a UML component diagram), and a suite of visual designers – including the *System Designer*, *Logical Datacenter Designer*, and *Deployment Designer* – that collectively addressed the task(s) otherwise undertaken by the UML deployment diagram; albeit with higher fidelity. I should also mention the *Class Designer t*hat provided Visual Studio developers with a UML-like class design experience that guaranteed no loss of information between the model and the code.

I documented these DSL-based software design / visual modeling tools in my co-authored book 'Professional Visual Studio 2005 Team System'.

Visual Studio 2010 Ultimate Edition

Fast forward to 2010, and in Visual Studio 2010 Ultimate Edition we have a more-or-less-complete suite of UML diagrams integrated natively into the Visual Studio IDE itself; complemented (if that's the right word) by the DSL-based *Class Designer a*nd the residual support for UML modeling in Visio.

This re-focusing on UML seems to have come about as a result of Microsoft defining its modeling strategy and joining the Object Management Group (OMG, the arbiter of UML) in 2008.

The end result of this evolution is that the overall Visual Studio 2010 UML offering is rather fragmented. Visio offers residual UML support that may be seen as complementary or in competition with the native UML support now offered within the Visual Studio IDE itself. The UML class diagram may be regarded as a strange bedfellow for the class-diagram-like *Class Designer* that was introduced with the *Visual Studio Team Editions*; the former being more UML compliant but less useful to developers who demand 100% synchronization between the model and the code. In order to address the issue of code generation from UML models (and some other issues) there is an optional add-on in the form of the Visualization and Modeling Feature Pack – see *Chapter 6 – Visualization and Modeling Feature Pack*. This may all leave Visual Studio users wondering how the various pieces of the jigsaw fit together, and in this book I hope to help answer that very question.

Summary

In this chapter you have learnt about the inclusion of UML, and the competitive or complementary (depending on your viewpoint) DSL approach, in Microsoft Visual Studio.

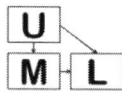

3 – Visual Studio 2010 UML for Analysts and Designers

In this chapter we'll look at the Visual Studio 2010 diagrams and features from the point of view of the business analyst or software designer, who will be analyzing a business problem and designing a software solution from scratch in a top-down fashion.

In Chapter 7 – Visio 2010 UML we'll look at how a developer might reverse engineer an existing software solution into Visio 2010.

For my running example I'll draw on one of the end-to-end UML modeling examples that I have used over the years in training courses, articles, and my previous UML book. While the underlying example is not entirely new, the coverage here in the context of Visual Studio 2010 *is* entirely new.

Visual Studio 2010 Modeling Project

Our starting point is to fire up Visual Studio 2010 Ultimate Edition and choose *New | Project* from the *File* menu, and then to choose the *Modeling Projects* project template. Since my example will be that of an order processing system, I choose to name the project OrderProcessingUML.

I can add my first UML diagram, and subsequent diagrams, by right-clicking the OrderProcessingUML project in the newly-created Visual Studio solution; and then by choosing *Add | New Item* from the context menu that appears. I can choose from the diagram types shown in *Figure 3 Add a UML Diagram*.

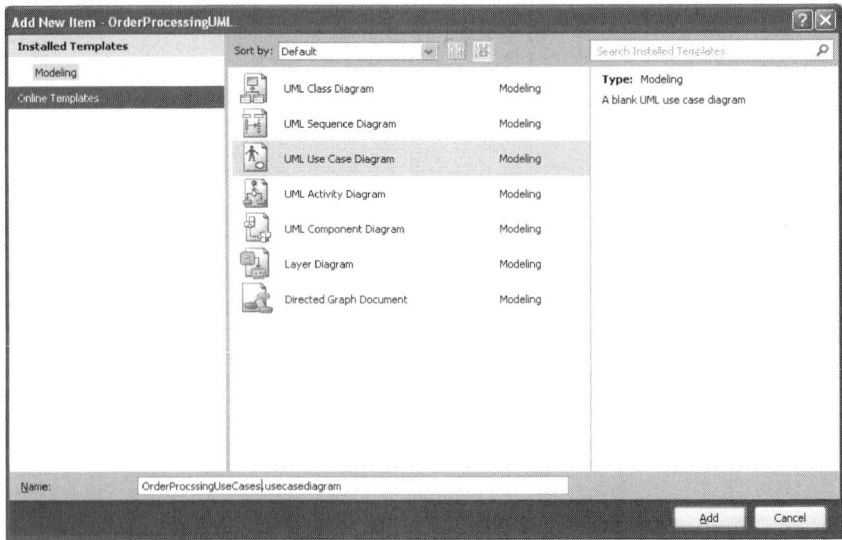

Figure 3 Add a UML Diagram

Notice that five of the diagrams are prefixed with 'UML' because they are UML-compliant diagrams. The other two diagrams that are not formally UML diagrams are documented in *Chapter 5 – Visual Studio 2010 UML for Developers*.

A note about UML Models and Diagrams

When working with UML diagrams, the first thing to note is that each diagram is a view of the underlying model, but is not the UML model itself. When you add new items to a diagram, these also become available as entities in the *UML Model Explorer* window that you can subsequently drag onto other diagrams.

If you don't see the UML Model Explorer in Visual Studio, you can access it from the Windows items of the Architecture menu.

The distinction between a diagram and 'the model' means that an Order object class may be the same entity no matter how many diagrams it appears on; and no matter whether it appears on a class diagram (to show its static relationships to other classes) or on a sequence diagram (to show how it interacts with other objects in the realization of a particular use case).

In this book I assume that you are sufficiently experienced with Visual Studio and / or other development environments and drawing tools to figure out how to click and drag items, how to modify their names on the diagrams, and how to connect two diagram items using a connector item.

> You should be able to find a handy guide to basic UML drawing tasks at http://msdn.microsoft.com/en-us/library/dd409405.aspx

UML Use Case Diagram

The logical starting point for a UML model is the use case diagram that illustrates user requirements, and in *Figure 3 Add a UML Diagram* you can see that I have already selected *UML Use Case Diagram* and named it OrderProcessingUseCases (.usecasediagram).

In *Figure 4 Use Case Diagram Toolbox* you can see that the toolbox allows me to drag various UML elements onto the diagram, and that I have already dragged an *Actor* onto the diagram. The complete set of UML elements shown are:

Actor: is a person or other entity – e.g. another software system – that makes use of the functions provided by the software solution.

Use Case: is a unit of functionality provided by the software solution to one or more actors.

Comment: is descriptive text that you can add to a diagram.

Subsystem: is a grouping of related use cases that may be implemented together to provide part of the overall functionality.

Artifact: is typically used to link a use case to an artifact such as a use case specification or a 'use case realization' sequence diagram.

Association: is a link between an actor and a use case showing that the particular actor performs a particular function.

Dependency: is a more generic version of the *Include* and *Extend* relationships described below, which link one use case to another.

Include: is a relationship between use cases to show that one use case makes use of the (reusable) functionality provided by another use case.

Extend: is a relationship between use cases to show that one use case provides an optional extension to the main use case functionality.

Generalization: is a relationship showing that one or more use cases are variations on a common theme.

Comment Link: allows you to indicate the diagram element to which a comment relates.

UML Software Design with Visual Studio 2010

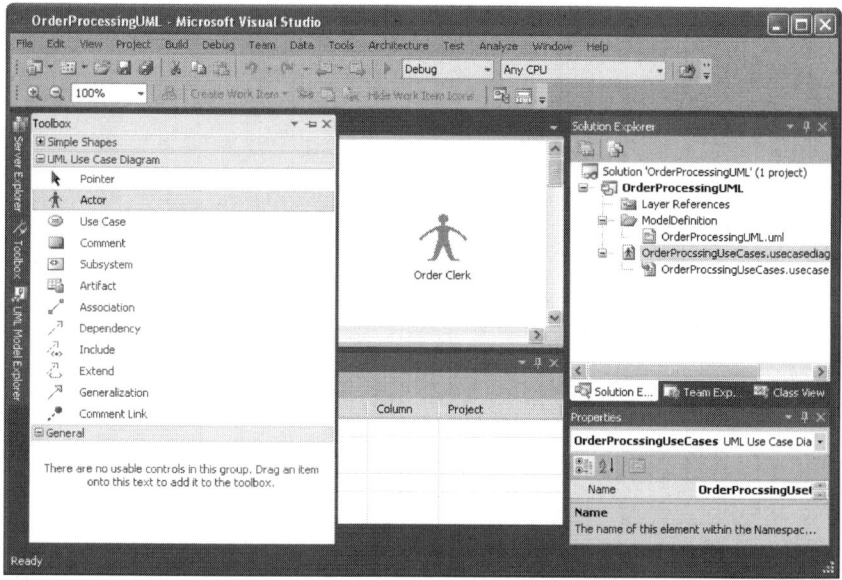

Figure 4 Use Case Diagram Toolbox

You should be able to find more details of these toolbox items at http://msdn.microsoft.com/en-us/library/dd409427.aspx

Example Use Case Diagram

In *Figure 5 Order Processing Use Case Diagram* I have provided an example use case diagram showing the various UML elements in their proper contexts. The UML elements *Actor, Use Case, Subsystem* and *Comment* are placed simply by clicking the required element in the toolbox and then clicking on the diagram surface. The remaining 'connector' UML elements are placed by clicking the required element in the toolbox, and then clicking on existing elements in turn on the diagram surface. Where a *Subsystem* is used, you should ensure that the relevant *Use Case* elements are placed onto the *Subsystem*, or dragged to it from another part of the diagram.

In this diagram:

- The overall software solution is divided into Ordering, Logistics, and Accounts subsystems; these subsystems representing the major areas of functionality that may be developed and delivered separately. An additional Common subsystem encapsulates functionality that may be useful across the other subsystems.

- The Ordering subsystem provides a use case for the Order Clerk actor to Take Order. This is a generalized use case that has two specializations – Take Telephone Order and Take Counter Order – that differ subtly in the sense that a Counter Order (i.e. one taken over-the-counter in the store) requires a credit card PIN to be entered into a device whereas a telephone order does not. In either case, the Take Order use case is also extended by an optional Mark for Special Delivery use case.

- The Logistics subsystem provides a use case for the Stock Picker actor to Pick Stock (from the warehouse) and a use case for the Delivery Man actor to Deliver Items. Since both use cases require the actor to first choose an order, the Choose Order use case is included from the Common subsystem.

- The Accounts subsystem provides a use case for the Accountant to Prepare Invoice (which requires the Choose Order functionality) and to Send Invoice (which does not).

UML Software Design with Visual Studio 2010

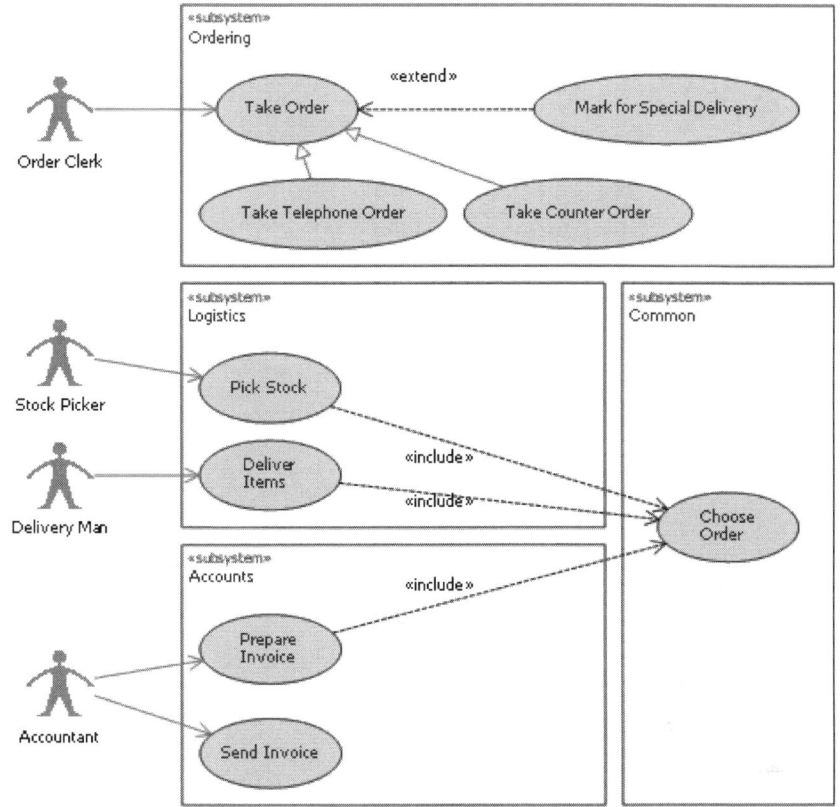

Figure 5 Order Processing Use Case Diagram

> **UML Style Tips**: Give actors *role names* not *job titles*, and *begin use case names with a strong verb.*

Notable by its absence on my diagram is the generic *Dependency* relationship between use cases, because in most situations the more specialized *Include* and *Extend* relationships are preferable. In a more generic sense we could theoretically link two use cases with a *Dependency* to show that one piece of functionality requires another piece of functionality to pre-exist. For example, the Deliver Items use case may be totally useless in a system with no ability to first Take Order, as shown in *Figure 6 Use Case Generic Dependency*. Taken to its logical conclusion, we might even consider stereotyping this dependency with a new kind of UML stereotype named <<requires>>. How useful this contrived example will be to you in practice may be a matter for debate, and to pull of this trick you would need to understand *UML Profiles* detailed in *4 – Best Practices and the Software Development Process*.

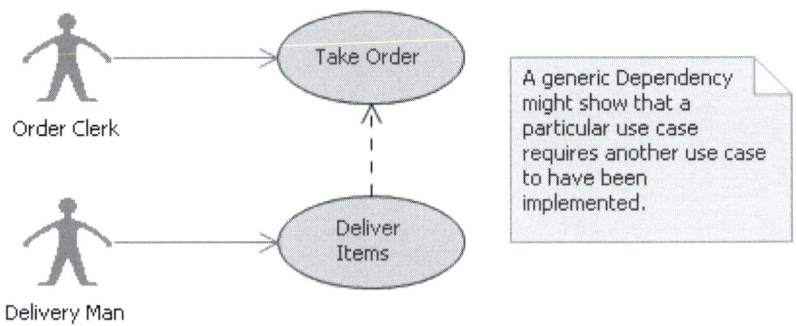

Figure 6 Use Case Generic Dependency

In this figure you will notice that I have also included a *Comment*, which is not connected to any other element. I have done this merely so that I have used each UML element at least once in this example.

About Use Case Specifications

Each use case on the use case diagram would typically be backed by a full use case specification – a written statement detailing the pre-conditions (what must be true before the use case is performed), the sequence of events (a textual equivalent of the sequence diagrams discussed next), and the post-conditions (what must be true after the use case has completed).

You might create and manage these use case specifications using a ˙ted tool; or you might store these specifications – one per use ˙˙osoft Word documents or web pages, in which case you could use the hyperlink property of the *Artifact* toolbox item in order to link a use case directly to its specification document.

You would access the hyperlink property via the Properties window in Visual Studio.

UML Sequence Diagram

Referring back to *Figure 3 Add a UML Diagram*, I now add a *UML Sequence Diagram* to the solution and name it Pick Stock. A sequence diagram is a UML interaction diagram that shows how objects interact in order to provide the functionality described by the use case. It provides a use case *realization*.

UML Model Explorer and the Toolbox

There are two ways to add items to a diagram: drag them from the *UML Model Explorer* (for pre-existing items) or add them from the *Toolbox* (for new items). If the UML Model Explorer is not visible, you can launch it by selecting *UML Model Explorer* from the *Windows* item of the *Architecture* menu in Visual Studio.

In my example, the only pre-existing item that I will drag from the *UML Model Explorer* is the Stock Picker actor.

All other UML elements will be selected from the toolbox shown in *Figure 7 Sequence Diagram Toolbox*. The toolbox items are as follow:

Lifeline: represents the length of time that an object participates in the sequence of interactions.

Synchronous: represents a message from one object to another that expects a return before execution continues.

Asynchronous: represents a message from one object to another that does not expect a return before execution continues.

Create: represents a new object instance being created by invoking its constructor method.

Comment: is descriptive text that you can add to a diagram.

Comment Link: allows you to indicate the diagram element to which a comment relates.

Interaction Use: encloses a sequence of messages that are defined in another diagram.

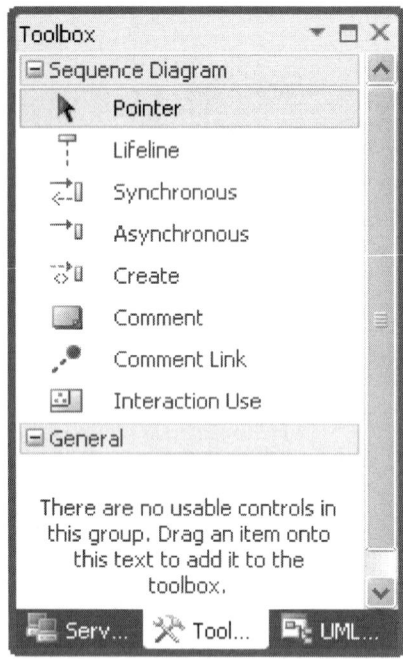

Figure 7 Sequence Diagram Toolbox

> You should be able to find out more about the items available in the sequence diagram toolbox at http://msdn.microsoft.com/en-us/library/dd409377.aspx

Creating the Sequence Diagram, Step-by-Step

My first step in creating a sequence diagram for the Pick Stock use case – after adding the Stock Picker actor from the *UML Model Explorer*, that is – is to drag a *Lifeline* element from the toolbox onto the diagram surface. Since I have not yet defined any object classes in this UML model, I need to *Create Class* from the context menu (right-click the *Lifeline*) as shown in *Figure 8 Create Class for Lifeline*.

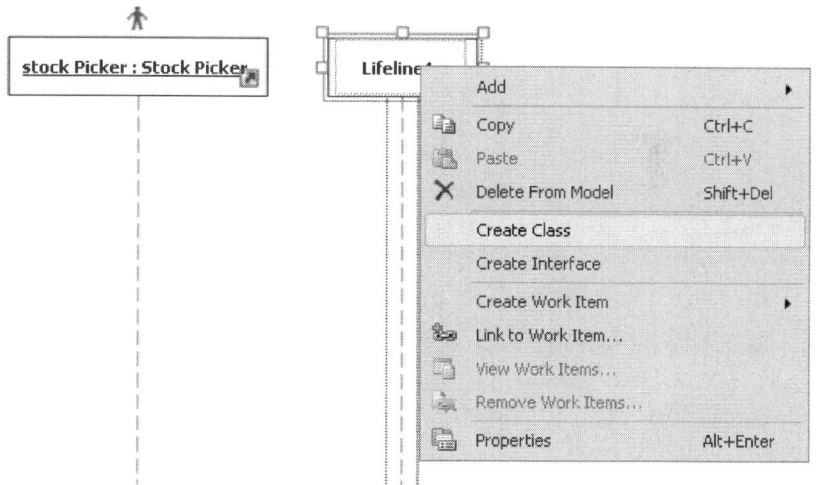

Figure 8 Create Class for Lifeline

The *UML Model Explorer* now contains a new class named Lifeline1, which I rename to PickStockController using the Visual Studio *Properties* window as shown in *Figure 9 Rename Class in Properties Window*.

If you're curious about why I named this class in the way that I did, it's because I intend this interaction to follow a Model-View-Controller (MVC) design pattern in which the flow of each use case is orchestrated by a dedicated controller class.

Tony Loton

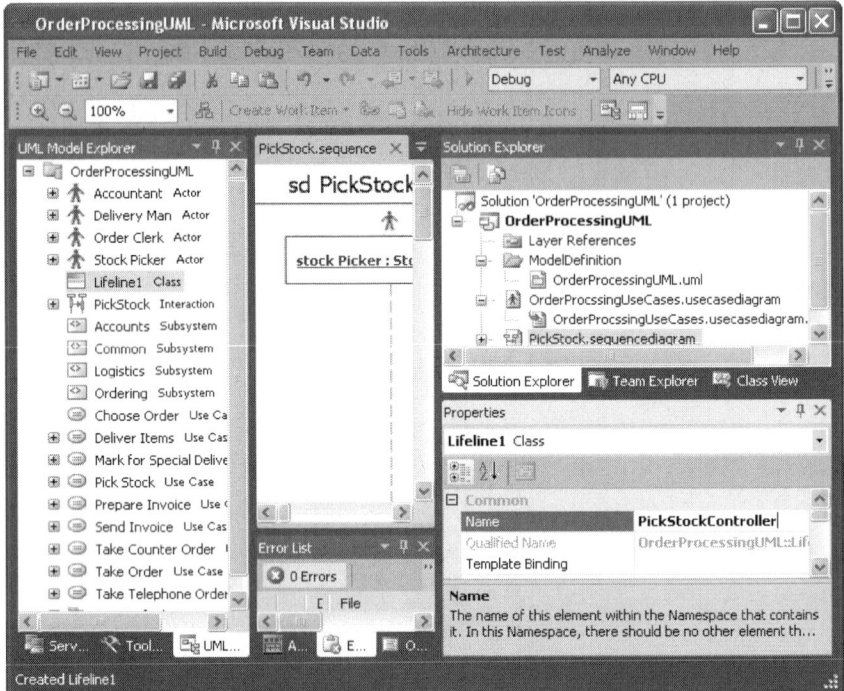

Figure 9 Rename Class in Properties Window

Next I use the *Synchronous* item from the toolbox to create a message line from the Stock Picker actor to the new PickStockController lifeline, and in the *Properties* window I name this message 'run'. But I do more than this, by also adding an *operation* named 'run' to the PickStockController in the *UML Model Explorer* and selecting this as the operation in the *Properties* window. All of this is shown in *Figure 10 Add Message and Operation*.

Pure business analysts might find it sufficient simply to give descriptive names to the messages that flow between object lifelines; but software designers and developers will want to show in concrete terms the operation that is invoked on the object that receives the message, and in this way will begin to build up the list of operations (or 'responsibilities') for each object class.

UML Software Design with Visual Studio 2010

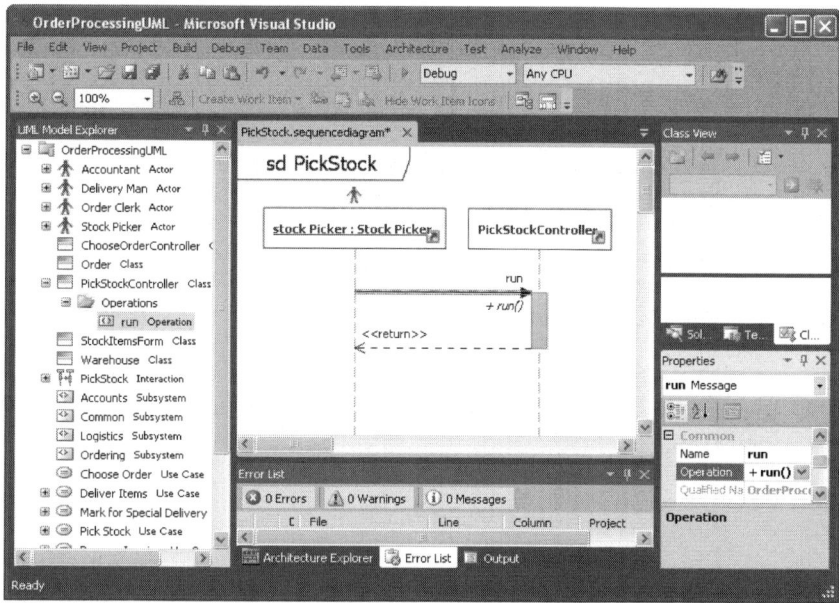

Figure 10 Add Message and Operation

Although I have added both a message name and an operation to the message shown in the previous figure, in the remainder of this example I will concentrate solely on *operations*.

In *Figure 11 Pick Stock Sequence Diagram* you can see my complete sequence diagram for the Pick Stock use case. The sequence of interactions is as follows:

1. First, the Stock Picker actor causes the run() operation to be invoked on the PickStockController object, presumably as a result of pressing a button or selecting a menu option.

2. Next, the PickStockController invokes the *ChooseOrder()* operation of the ChooseOrderController, the result of which is a chosenOrder being returned to the PickStockController. Choosing an order is in itself a non-trivial interaction that I

39

have simply referenced in this sequence diagram using an *Interaction Use* item from the sequence diagram toolbox. Double-clicking the 'interaction use' box labeled Choose Order would take us to the sequence diagram for the Choose Order use case, and in this way I am modeling the <<include>> relationship between the Pick Stock and Choose Order use cases shown in *Figure 5 Order Processing Use Case Diagram*.

3. After receiving the actor's chosenOrder as the return value from the ChooseOrderController, the PickStockController invokes the display() operation of the StockItemsForm. At this point I would like to have shown an *Asynchronous* message from the actor to the StockItemsForm, to show that the actor interacts with the form, but due to technical difficulties (it doesn't seem to be possible in Visual Studio) I have instead used a *Comment* labeled 'select stock item' along with a *Comment Link* to show the user interaction with the form.

4. Having received the actor's chosen stockItem as a return value from the StockItemsForm, the PickStockController invokes the allocateStock(stockItem) operation on the chosenOrder:Order object so as to allocate the stock item to the order.

5. Finally, the same stockItem is removed from warehouse stock by invoking the removeItem(stockItem) operation on the Warehouse.

UML Software Design with Visual Studio 2010

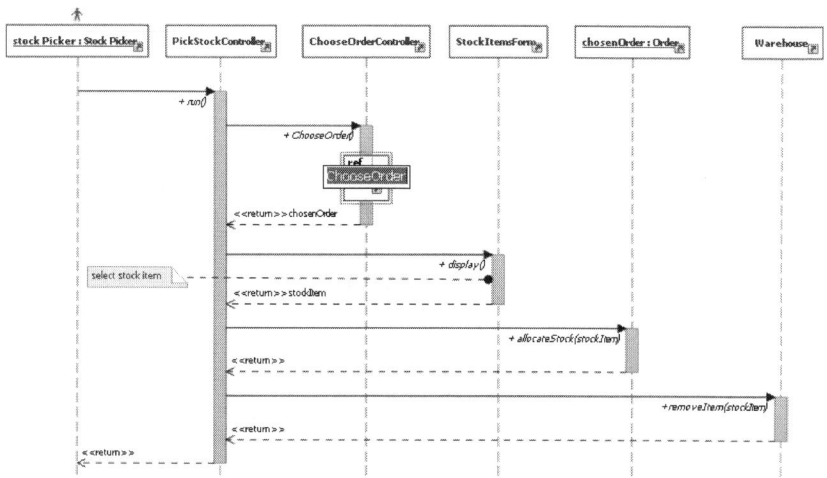

Figure 11 Pick Stock Sequence Diagram

UML Style Tip: *Strive for left-to-right ordering of messages.*

While the foregoing numbered points describe the sequence of interactions, a few additional notes may be required for a complete understanding of this diagram.

Sequence Diagram Additional Notes

These notes refer to more detailed aspects of the diagram shown in *Figure 11 Pick Stock Sequence Diagram*.

<u>Interaction Use</u>

In my sequence diagram I have included an *Interaction Use* named Choose Order that links to another sequence diagram showing more details of how the ChooseOrder() operation of the ChooseOrderController works. In *Figure 12 Interaction Use* you can see that by right-clicking this interaction use on the diagram I can use the context menu to *Go To Sequence* and view the linked sequence diagram. Alternatively, I can *Link To Sequence* so as to re-link this interaction use to any other sequence diagram I wish – which is how I linked it to my Choose Order sequence diagram in the first place.

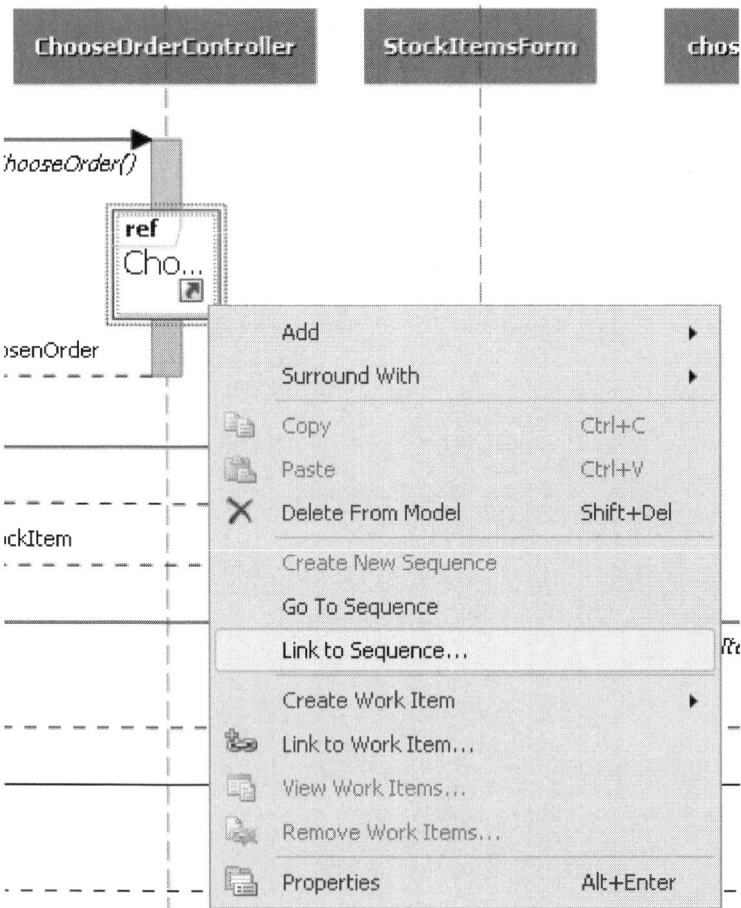

Figure 12 Interaction Use

Object Class and Instance Lifelines

You will notice that some object lifelines in the diagram are labeled with only a class name such as StockItemsForm. In these cases the specific instance of the object class is not important, and may not even exist in cases where class-level operations are invoked. Notice how the chosenOrder in the <<return>> chosenOrder message from the ChooseOrderController to the PickStockController corresponds with the naming of the Order lifeline as chosenOrder:Order. The Order lifeline represents the specific chosenOrder returned in the earlier step.

You can give an object lifeline a particular instance name by clicking the lifeline and then editing its *Name* in the *Properties* Window, and this may be particularly useful when you need to distinguish two instances of the same class on a single sequence diagram. Imagine the sequence diagram from a Transfer Funds use case in a banking application; in which you would need to show a sourceAccount:BankAccount and a destinationAccount:BankAccount.

Modifying Messages and Operation Signatures

Synchronous messages are always concluded with a <<return> message that is labeled as such, and you can modify the message *Name* in the Visual Studio *Properties* window to become (for example) <<return>> chosenOrder or <<return>> stockItem.

Whenever you add an operation to a class in the *UML Model Explorer*, as I did in *Figure 10 Add Message and Operation* so as to make this operation available for selection as a message on the sequence diagram, you can also specify a more comprehensive operation *Signature* in the Properties window as shown in *Figure 13 Operation Signature in the Properties Window*. This is how I made two of the sequence diagram messages read *allocateStock(stockItem)* and *removeItem(stockItem)* respectively.

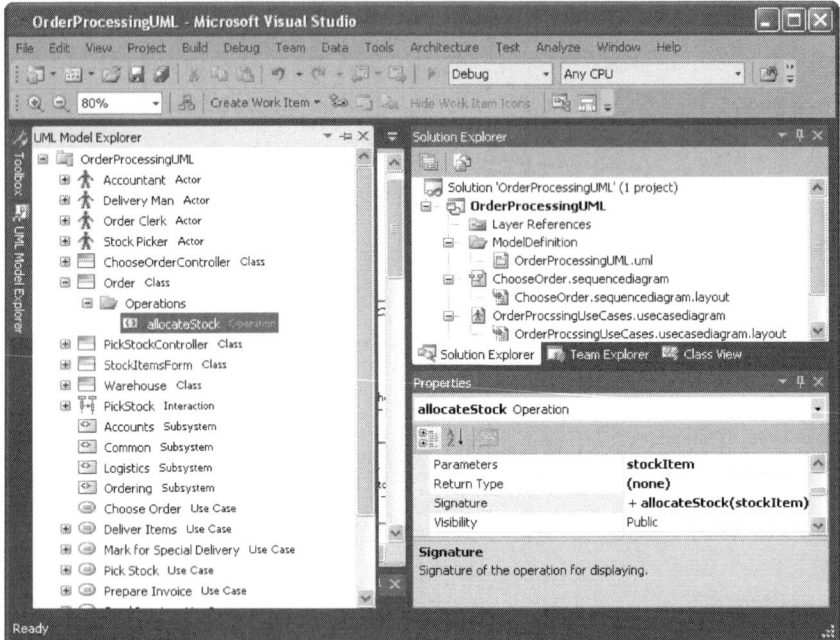

Figure 13 Operation Signature in the Properties Window

Adding Sequence Diagram Items from the UML Model Explorer

In this example I have created new object classes as needed by dragging an *Object Lifeline* onto the diagram, right-clicking, and choosing *Create Class* from the context menu. It is also possible to create object classes in advance in the *UML Model Explorer*, and drag these pre-defined classes onto the sequence diagram.

UML Class Diagram

After creating the Pick Stock sequence diagram, my next step is to create a *Class Diagram* showing the relationships between the object classes that participate in this sequential realization of the Pick Stock use case. So, I create the PickStockParticipatingClasses.classdiagram.

UML Software Design with Visual Studio 2010

The toolbox for the *Class Diagram* is show in *Figure 14 Class Diagram Toolbox*, and the definitions of the various items are as follows.

Class: represents an object class.

Interface: represents an interface that may be implemented by a class.

Enumeration: defines a list of specific values.

Package: represents a container for types (classes, interfaces etc.) and other packages, rather like a folder or directory structure.

Comment: is descriptive text that you can add to a diagram.

Association: represents a potentially persistent relationship between two object classes.

Aggregation: represents a stronger form of *Association*, as a whole-part or container-contained relationship between two classes.

Composition: represents an even stronger form of *Association*, in which the whole-part relationship is potentially immutable.

Dependency: shows that one class is dependent on (i.e. makes use of) another class without necessarily being associated with it in any persistent sense.

Inheritance: shows that a type (a class or an interface) inherits behavior and / or attributes from a base type.

Package Import: specifies that a package imports types defined in another package.

Connector: creates a default relationship between elements, based on the kinds of elements being connected.

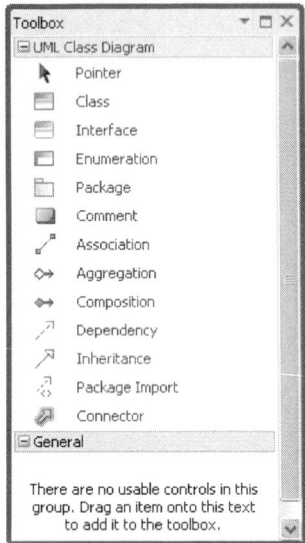

Figure 14 Class Diagram Toolbox

> You should be able to find out more about the class diagram toolbox items at http://msdn.microsoft.com/en-us/library/dd409437.aspx

To begin the participating classes diagram I would have liked to have dragged the StockPicker actor from the UML Explorer onto the diagram. Over the years I have been able to do this kind of thing using other UML tools, because those tools treated actors as class-equivalent types. It's not such a big deal that I can't do this here, but it means that I can't show a notional dependency between the actor and the PickStockController class.

The PickStockController and many of the other classes required on this diagram were defined (at least partially) in the course of devising the sequence diagram for the realization of the Pick Stock use case, and they *can* be dragged from the UML Explorer. In *Figure 15 Pick Stock Participating Classes #1* I have used the toolbox (rather than the *UML Model Explorer*) to add a *new* Controller class to the diagram; and this class will act as a base class for all other controller classes. I have used *Inheritance* (otherwise know in UML as 'generalization') relationships to show that the PickStockController and ChooseOrderController classes inherit from the Controller base class. I have promoted the run() operation by adding it to the base class, so as to provide some default behavior for all controllers when they are run.

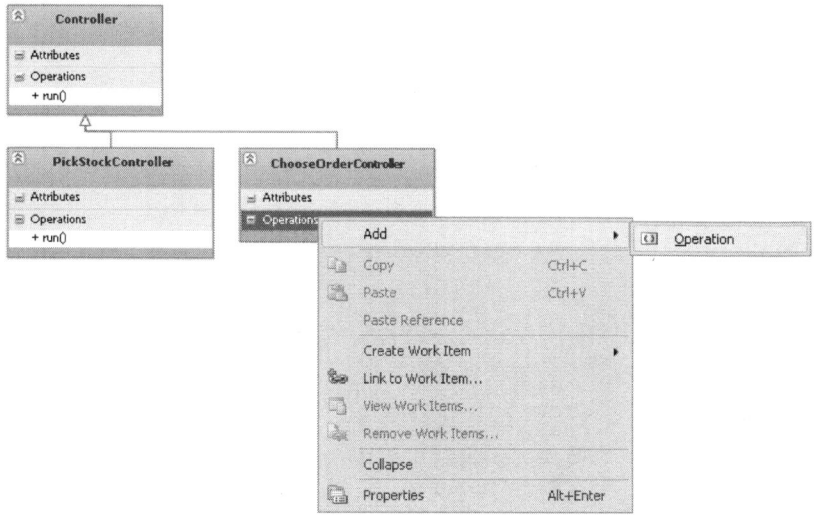

Figure 15 Pick Stock Participating Classes #1

As an alternative to adding a base class, I might have added a Controller *Interface* to the diagram and inherited from it in exactly the same way – to show that all controller classes must implement a run() operation.

Whereas the majority of operations may already be present on their respective classes (as a consequence of devising the sequence diagrams) this will not be true of an object's attributes. So I add them at this stage.

After adding a new attribute to a class, I would specify its visibility (*Public*, *Protected*, *Package* or *Private*) and its type (e.g. String) using the

Properties window as shown in *Figure 16 Specify Operation Visibility and Type*. You can see that on the Order class I have specified a *Public* attribute named orderNumber of type *Integer,* and a *Private* attribute named orderDate of type *String*.

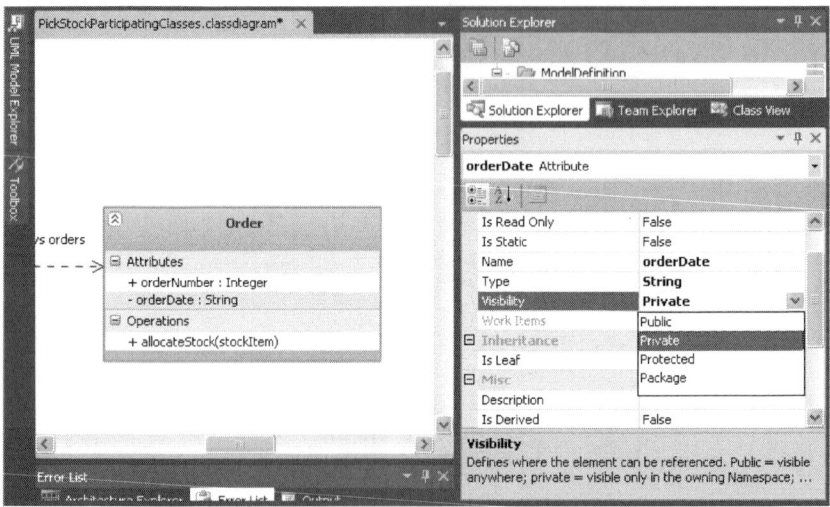

Figure 16 Specify Operation Visibility and Type

In the next step I add a new StockItem class by dragging a class item from the toolbox. I give this class two attributes – itemType and serialNumber – and I add an *Association* (from the toolbox) to this StockItem class from the Order class. In *Figure 17 Add Association* to Class Diagram you can see how I have used the *Properties* window to modify the role name (to 'orderedItem') and multiplicity (to '1..*') at the Order end of the association. Reading this association in English would yield the sentence "An Order is associated with one or more orderedItems of type StockItem."

UML Software Design with Visual Studio 2010

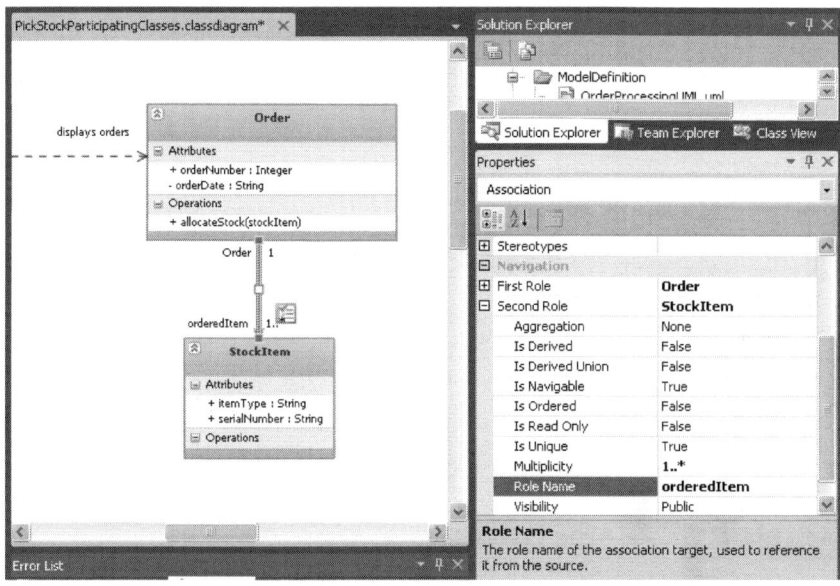

Figure 17 Add Association to Class Diagram

From a pure UML point of view I would have been tempted to add an 'association class' to this association, representing an object – let's call it StockAllocation – that exists only where a stockItem instance has been linked to an Order instance. As far as I can tell, Visual Studio 2010 UML does not allow association classes, but it's no big deal and I could use a regular class if the StockAllocation concept is important to me.

In the final class diagram shown in *Figure 18 Pick Stock Participating Classes*, notice the distinction between *Dependency* relationships and *Association* relationships; the former denoting that one class merely utilizes another class in a non-persistent sense, and the latter denoting that instances of two classes may form a persistent relationship as might be recorded in a database. The PickStockController 'depends on' the StockItemsForm and the Warehouse because it makes use of these classes in the Pick Stock use case; but there are no persistent (as recorded in a database) links between instances of these classes. In contrast an Order instance is 'associated' with one of more StockItem instances in a persistent sense, and this would be recorded in a database.

Notice also the *Aggregation* relationship showing that StockItems are contained within a Warehouse. In this aggregation I have used role names and an association name such that in plain English the relationship reads "A Warehouse (which is a 'location') holds stock of zero or more 'stockedItem'."

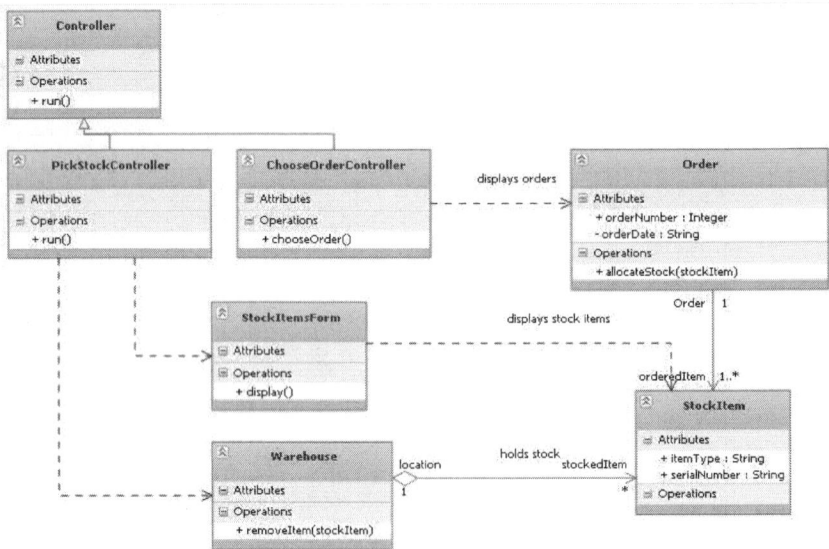

Figure 18 Pick Stock Participating Classes

> **UML Style Tip**: *Prefer complete singular nouns for class names: 'Order' rather than 'Orders'. Model a dependency when the relationship is transitory,* but *do not model every dependency.*

Note that although in this case I have drawn a class diagram to show the object classes that participate in a particular use case, class diagrams are not limited to this usage. You might draw a diagram to show the classes within a particular package or namespace of your solution, or (for a very small system) all of the classes on one diagram.

UML Activity Diagram

I have left this diagram type until now so as not to spoil the logical flow from the *Use Case Diagram*, through the *Sequence Diagram*, to the *Class Diagram*.

The *Activity Diagram* is rather like a traditional flowchart, and it may be useful at various stages of the modeling process: to describe the arrangement of use cases in an over-arching business process, to document the flow of a specific algorithm, or (as I'll suggest later) to model the behaviors of a specific object class in the form of a State-Chart diagram.

Figure 19 Activity Diagram Toolbox shows the UML elements available from the activity diagram toolbox, which are as follows:

Initial Node: marks the start of the activity sequence.

Activity Final Node: marks the end of the activity sequence.

Action: represents a single activity step within the overall sequence.

Object Node: is a node that can transmit, buffer, filter and transform objects.

Comment: allows you to add descriptive text to a diagram.

Decision Node: allows the activity flow to take alternative courses.

Merge Node: brings alternative activity flows together into a single outgoing flow.

Fork Node: shows where a single execution flow splits into several concurrent (parallel) threads.

Join Node: shows where several concurrent (parallel) threads synchronize into one thread of execution.

Send Signal Action: is an action node that sends a signal to another system or activity.

Accept Event Action: is an action that waits for a signal or event.

Call Behavior Action: is an action that calls another activity.

Call Operation Action: is an action that calls an operation.

Input Pin: allows data to flow into an action.

Output Pin: allows data to flow out of an action.

Activity Parameter Node: creates a parameter that conveys data into or out of the activity.

Connector: adds a connection or flow between elements on the diagram.

UML Software Design with Visual Studio 2010

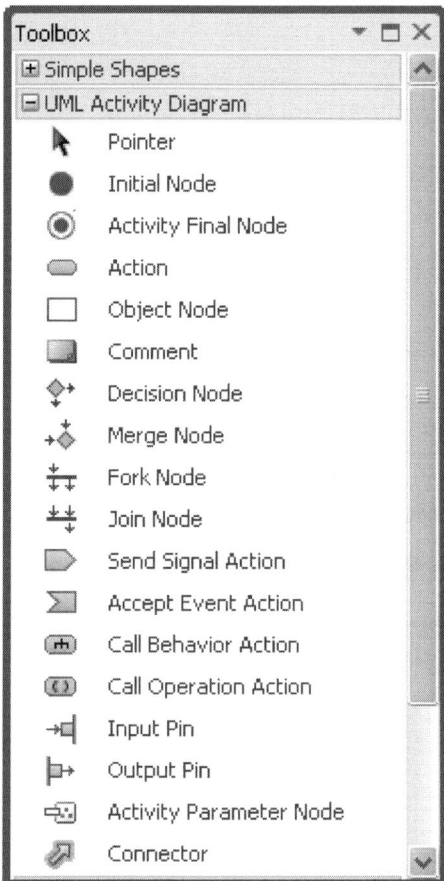

Figure 19 Activity Diagram Toolbox

> You should be able to find out more about these toolbox items at http://msdn.microsoft.com/en-us/library/dd409360.aspx

In *Figure 20 Example Activity Diagram* you can see my activity diagram for the overarching business process that comprises the use cases defined in *Figure 5 Order Processing Use Case Diagram*. Although I have left the discussion of activity diagrams until now, in *this context* it may well be the first diagram that you create – before the use case diagram.

The first step in the Order Processing business process (after the *Initial Node*) is the Take Order action that in this example directly represents the Take Order use case. This action has an *Output Pin* labeled newOrder showing how a new order (identified as sampleOrder) is created at this step.

In the next step a *Decision Node* decides whether this order will be a special delivery order; and if so, the Mark for Special Delivery action is performed. In this way I have modeled the scenario in which the Mark for Special Delivery extension of the Take Order use case (see *Figure 5 Order Processing Use Case Diagram)* is executed.

Whichever route is taken to this point – Mark for Special Delivery, or not – the next step is to Pick Stock. The *Input Pin* labeled selectedOrder shows how notionally the sampleOrder created in the Take Order step is now selected as the order for which stock is to be picked.

At this point, two subsequent actions can be taken in parallel as indicated by the *Fork Node*. There is nothing to prevent the DeliveryMan actor from performing the Deliver Items step at more or less the same time as the Accountant performs the Prepare Invoice function.

Whereas the two previous actions can be performed in parallel, both actions must have been completed before the next action – Print Invoice – can occur. In this final step – prior to the *Activity Final Node* – I have used a *Call Operation Action* to show how at this step we would invoke the printInvoice() operation on the Invoice class.

UML Software Design with Visual Studio 2010

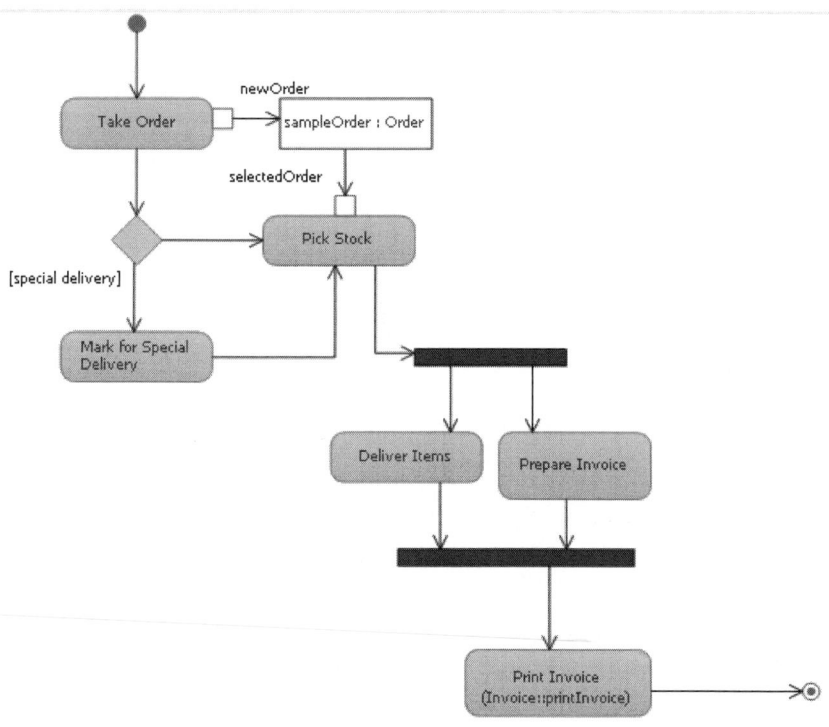

Figure 20 Example Activity Diagram

UML Style Tips: *Place the start point at the top-left corner,* and *include an end point.*

Note that where a particular action encapsulates a more detailed activity flow this can be modeled using the *Call Behavior Action* toolbox item. For example: the Pick Stock action might involve first selecting an order, and this non-trivial action may be described on another activity diagram that is referenced by a *Call Behavior Action*; in a similar way to how a more detailed Choose Order sequence diagram was referenced in *Figure 12 Interaction Use* using an *Interaction Use*.

I have arranged the activities roughly into columns corresponding with the actors that would perform the use cases represented by the activity actions. For example: the left-most column represents use cases performed by the Order Clerk actor; the right-most column represents use cases performed by the Accountant actor.

In dedicated UML tools, these columns would typically be represented explicitly as *swim lanes*; and while the Visual Studio 2010 UML activity diagrams do not support swim lanes as such, the prevailing guidance appears to be to simulate swim lanes using lines or rectangles from the *Simple Shapes* section of the toolbox.

When placing the *Object Node* on the diagram I specified both an instance name (sampleOrder) and type name (Order) using the *Properties* window as shown in *Figure 21 Object Instance on Activity Diagram*.

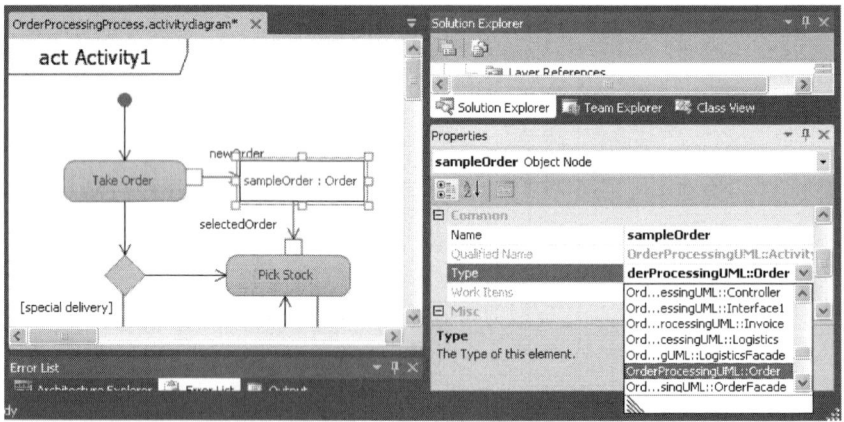

Figure 21 Object Instance on Activity Diagram

About State-Chart Diagrams

The majority of UML tools I used in the past supported state-chart diagrams that showed the various states in which a particular object exits, along with the actions that caused the object to transition from one state to another. But many of those tools did not explicitly support activity diagrams that showed the activities involved in a business process (or, if you like, the states in which the business process can exist and the actions that cause the process to transition from one activity – or state – to another).

I have deliberately used language to blur the distinction between state-chart diagrams and activity diagrams so as to make more credible the fact that I often used state-chart diagrams in the past as a substitute for activity diagrams. Imagine an object class representing the Order Processing business process, and imagine that the states of that hypothetical object represent the steps of the business process.

With Visual Studio 2010 the situation is exactly opposite: activity diagrams are supported, but state-chart diagrams are not; which raises the possibility of using an activity diagram in lieu of a state-chart diagram.

It's not ideal, but it is possible, as shown in *Figure 22 Order State-Chart Diagram*. This diagram shows that an Order object can exist in states Unpicked, Picked, Delivered, and Invoiced and that it transitions between these states on receipt of certain events (like allocateStock, deliver, and invoice) if certain conditions are met.

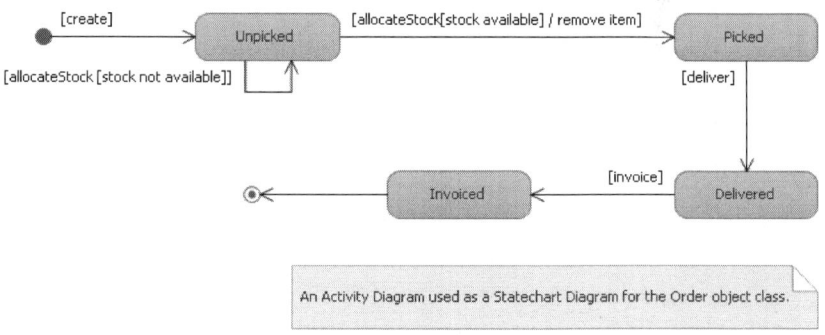

Figure 22 Order State-Chart Diagram

I have had to fudge this slightly because it appears that in Visual Studio 2010 each transition allows you to specify only a *Guard condition* whereas UML traditionally allows you to specify an *event*, a *condition*, and an *action* like this:

```
event [condition] / action
```

or (as a concrete example)…

```
allocateStock [stock available] / removeItem
```

I have simply entered this entire text as the *Guard* on a transition in my pseudo-state-chart diagram; and it works well enough as long as you ignore the superfluous outer braces on the transitions.

UML Component Diagram

The UML *Component Diagram* shows how a software system will be composed of a set of deployable components – assembly DLLs, executable files, or web services – that interact through well-defined interfaces and which have their internal details hidden.

In this running example I create a new component diagram and name it OrderProcessingComponents.componentdiagram.

You can add items to a component diagram by dragging them from the toolbox shown in *Figure 23 Component Diagram Toolbox*. The items available in the toolbox are:

Component: is a deployable and potentially replaceable unit of system functionality.

Dependency: shows that one component depends on another component.

Delegation: connects an external interface on a component to an interface that provides the required functionality on a contained component.

UML Software Design with Visual Studio 2010

Provided Interface: defines an interface provided by a component.

Required Interface: defines an interface that must be provided to a component by another component.

Comment: allows you to add descriptive text to a diagram.

Generalization: specifies that one component inherits features and behaviors from another component.

Connector: allows you to connect two elements, such as a *Provider Interface* to a *Required Interface*.

Part Assembly: specifies a connection between parts within a component.

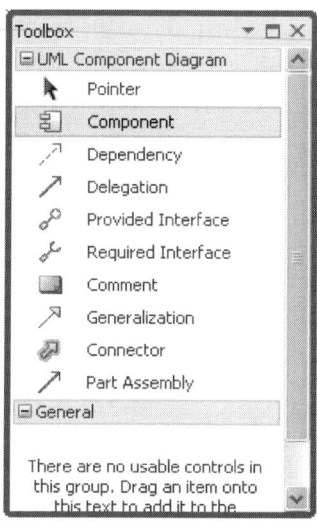

Figure 23 Component Diagram Toolbox

You should be able to see more details of these toolbox items at http://msdn.microsoft.com/en-us/library/dd409390.aspx

My example component diagram is shown in *Figure 24 Example Component Diagram*. In the diagram I have added components stereotyped as <<subsystem>> to represent each of the subsystems defined originally in *Figure 5 Order Processing Use Case Diagram*. Each of these represents a deployable application, and so each one inherits from a generic WebApplication component via a Generalization relationship. As defined originally in the use case diagram, the Logistics and Accounts subsystems require reusable functionality to ChooseOrder, and I have modeled this requirement by adorning each of these subsystems with a ChooseOrderProxy *Required Interface*. These requirements are satisfied by the ChooseOrderFacade *Provided Interface* on the Common component, which in turn has a *Delegate* to the ChooseOrderInterface *Provided Interface* on the Order contained component. Since the OrderingApp *Component* depends on the Common *Component* (because it uses some of the constituent entities – not shown – even though it uses none of the explicit interfaces) I have modeled this as a simple *Dependency*.

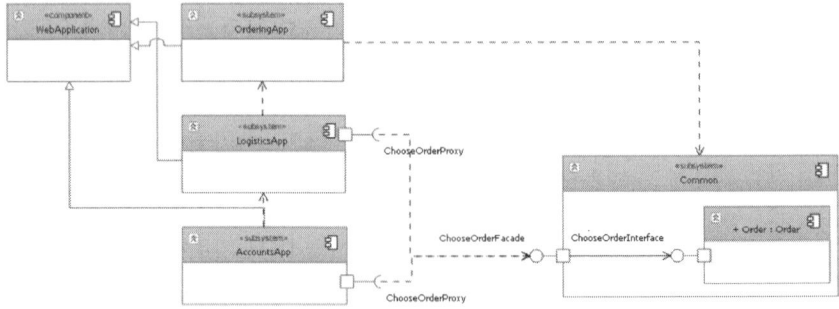

Figure 24 Example Component Diagram

UML Style Tips: *Prefer left-hand side for (provided) interfaces*, and *make components dependent only on interfaces*.

Bear in mind that I have contrived this component diagram so as to include as many UML elements as possible, and it is therefore not necessarily an example of optimal design.

In the contract-first design approach we would specify component interfaces before concerning ourselves with implementation details.

What's missing in Visual Studio 2010 UML?

I need to be careful when stating what is missing, for several reasons: an apparently missing feature might be included under a different name, it might be introduced in the future (by the time you read this), or I might simply have missed it. In short, it is difficult to prove that something doesn't exist. But here are some of the things that I believe to be missing at the time of writing.

UML connoisseurs will already have spotted that at least three UML diagram types are missing from the list of diagram types shown in *Figure 3 Add a UML Diagram*. In the Visual Studio 2010 Ultimate Edition that I have used to write this book, the common UML diagram types known as *Collaboration Diagrams*, *State-Chart Diagrams*, and *Deployment Diagrams* are conspicuous by their absence.

In the case of collaboration diagrams, this may be a minor irritation to UML aficionados but is no big thing because sequence diagrams provide exactly the same information – albeit in a different visual form.

In the case of state-chart diagrams, in *Figure 22 Order State-Chart Diagram* you saw how I attempted to simulate this diagram type using the similar *Activity Diagram*.

In the case of deployment diagrams: this may be an oversight, it may be on the way in a future version, or it may be that the same purpose is achieved adequately by the Team System *Deployment Designer* or by the Visual Studio 2010 architectural *Layer Diagram*.

One can dig deeper to find other omissions and anomalies; such as the lack of support for 'association classes' in UML class diagrams and the apparent lack of swim lanes in UML activity diagrams. These features may be supported in future versions, or may be regarded as obsolete, and in any case are generally easy enough to work around.

One can dig even deeper into the UML meta-model and notice that in Visual Studio 2010 actors appear not to be regarded as classifiers like regular classes. Which means that you can't place them 'participating' class diagrams; but you might never have considered doing this.

From UML to Code

Many software analysts and designers will use UML simply to model a business problem and the corresponding software solution from a pure conceptual perspective. But software designers and developers will want to make the leap from a conceptual UML design to concrete code artifacts.

The current Visual Studio 2010 UML feature set does not lend itself to the automatic generation of code from UML, and this is perhaps the weakest aspect… currently. All is not lost, and you will find some additional guidance on generating code from UML (or UML-like) models in *Chapter 5 – Visual Studio 2010 UML for Developers* and *Chapter 6 – Visualization and Modeling Feature Pack*. But in the next chapter we'll stay at the conceptual level by looking at best practices for structuring UML models and for enacting a UML-driven software development process.

Summary

In this chapter you have learnt about the five UML diagrams included in the Visual Studio 2010 Ultimate Edition. The focus in this chapter has been on conceptual analysis and design.

UML Software Design with Visual Studio 2010

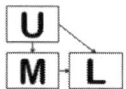

4 – Best Practices and the Software Development Process

Using UML tools is all well and good, but we also need to know how to use these tools – and the notation – effectively in the context of a software development process. In this chapter I aim to introduce some of the software development best practices that are related to the use of UML; not by any means exhaustively, but as a springboard for your further reading and research. I also use this chapter as a catch-all for some of the features not yet discussed; starting with…

How to Copy and Paste UML Diagrams

If you're using you UML to communicate your design ideas you will of course want to take your diagrams out of the Visual Studio environment and into another product like Microsoft Word or PowerPoint. And you might want to simply print them out.

One approach is to press the CTRL + PRNT SCRN keys to capture a screenshot into the clipboard, and then paste and crop the result in another application; which is pretty much how I produced the figures for this book.

A better approach is to select all the items on a diagram by pressing CTRL + A, and then pasting into another application. If you want to copy and paste only some of the diagram elements, you can hold down the CTRL key while clicking on the required elements, and then paste into the other application. This is how I produced the partial class diagram shown in *Figure 25 Partial Class Diagram*, which shows a subset of the diagram first shown in *Figure 18 Pick Stock Participating Classes*.

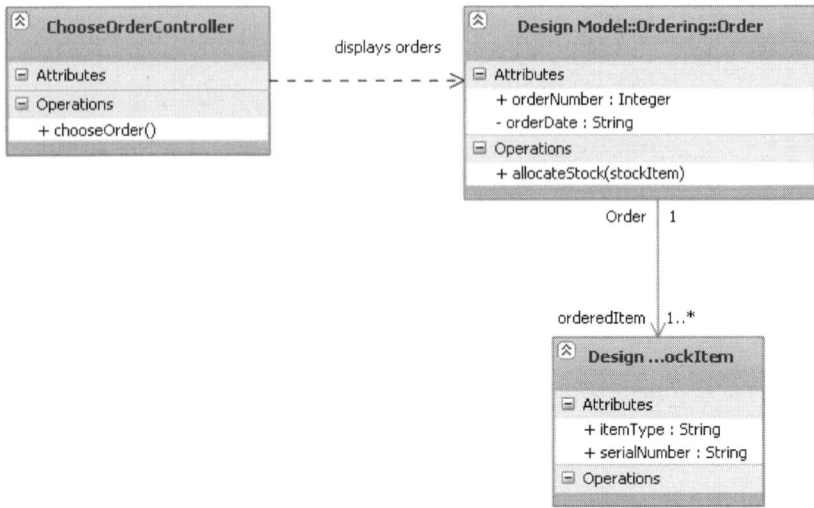

Figure 25 Partial Class Diagram

If you want to export diagrams programmatically, for example as a custom documentation generation utility, then it is possible to do so with some clever programming. It's beyond the scope of this book, but you should be able to find details of how to do just this at the following web addresses:

http://msdn.microsoft.com/en-us/library/ff469815.aspx

http://msdn.microsoft.com/en-us/library/dd554948%28VS.100%29.aspx

http://blogs.msdn.com/b/camerons/archive/2010/03/08/save-a-diagram-to-image-file.aspx

UML Notation Style Guidelines

The developers among you will be familiar with coding standards that assure consistent coding style across the entire development team. Once such coding standard might be to use 'Pascal case' (e.g. InvoiceOrder) rather than 'camel case' (e.g. invoiceOrder) for the names of an object's operations. Yes, I know I'm guilty of breaking this rule, but it's a very language-specific rule and sometimes a matter of preference. The whys and wherefores of which style is best can run and run, but what is important is *consistency*.

You might wonder if there are any such standards for drawing UML diagrams, and in this respect you might take a look at Scott Ambler's book "Elements of UML Style" published by Cambridge Press. While I don't agree with every piece of advice in the book, it does at least provide a good starting point for thinking about drawing UML diagrams with consistency and clarity.

The advice in Amber's book ranges from the general – avoid crossing lines on diagrams, and make each diagram fit on a single printed page – to the specific: begin use case names with a strong verb. You will have seen a few *UML Style Tips* included where appropriate in the preceding chapters of the book you are reading now.

UML Profiles and Stereotypes

The various examples in the previous chapter have *incidentally* demonstrated the use of UML stereotypes that make the same UML element or relationship mean something slightly different in different contexts. For example: you have seen use case relationships stereotyped as <<include>> or <<extend>>, and you have seen components stereotyped as <<subsystem>>.

Which stereotypes are available to you for each UML element is determined by which UML profile you choose. In *Figure 26 UML Profiles* I have selected my Analysis Model package (see next section) in *UML Model Explorer* and in the *Properties* window I have ensured that the *C# Profile* is unselected for this package; so that C# stereotypes cannot be used in my analysis model. For my Implementation Model (also shown in the figure) I might select the *C# Profile*, which would allow me (for example) to stereotype a class as a *C# Class* thereby allowing me access to C#-specific attributes like *Is Partial* and *Is Static*.

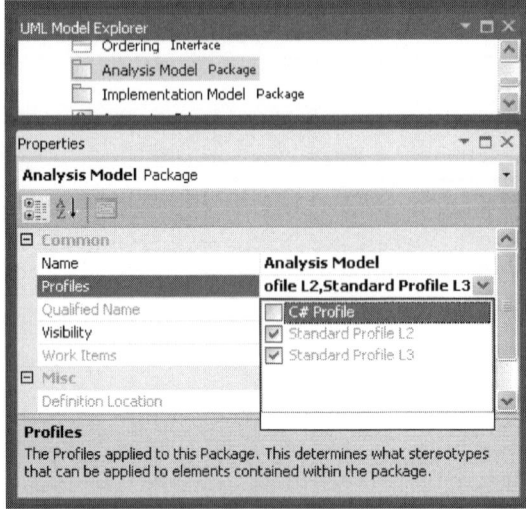

Figure 26 UML Profiles

Although it is beyond the scope of this book, I should mention that it is possible to extend the set of available UML Profiles by creating your own profiles containing your own stereotypes. Navigate to the following folder (it may be slightly different for your Visual Studio installation)...

```
C:\Program Files\Microsoft Visual Studio 10.0\Common7\IDE\Extensions\Microsoft\Architecture Tools\UmlProfiles
```

...and you will see the following files listed, each one corresponding with the profiles shown in *Figure 26 UML Profiles*.

```
CSharp.Profile
StandardProfileL2.Profile
StandardProfileL3.Profile
```

These are eXtensible Markup Language (XML) files, of which you could create one of your own. For example, you might include database stereotypes such as <<table>>.

You would then make your new profile available by editing the `extension.vsixmanifest` file that is located in the same folder.

UML Software Design with Visual Studio 2010

You should be able to discover more about creating a custom UML profile for Visual Studio 2010 at the following web address:

http://msdn.microsoft.com/en-us/library/dd465143%28VS.100%29.aspx

Structuring the Model

As created in the previous chapter, my model is rather one-dimensional because all of the object classes have been created in what one might call the 'root folder' of the UML model. In reality we would want to structure the model by arranging the classes into packages (like sub-folders) according to how closely coupled they are.

This is similar to organizing classes into namespaces, but it need not be the same. There might be a one-to-one correspondence between packages and namespaces, and then again there might not.

One logical arrangement of classes into packages in my running example would be for the package structure to mirror the decomposition of the software solution into use case subsystems (see *Figure 5 Order Processing Use Case Diagram*) which was also mirrored in the decomposition into components (see *Figure 24 Example Component Diagram*).

In *Figure 27 Class Package Structure* you can see that I have created three packages in the *UML Model Explorer* named Accounts, Logistics, and Ordering, and I have moved some of my previously-created classes into appropriate packages by cutting and pasting within the *UML Model Explorer*. I have also created a new high level class diagram to show how my new packages are interrelated: the Logistics package depends on the Ordering package (because you can't allocate stock and deliver an order without an Order), and the Accounts package depends on the Logistics package (because you can't raise an invoice unless an order has been fulfilled). These package dependencies give us a clue as to the order in which our classes must be implemented.

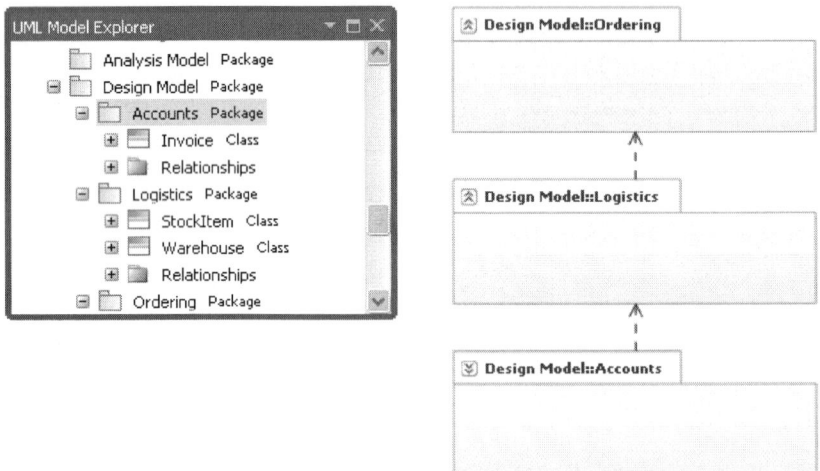

Figure 27 Class Package Structure

UML Style Tip: *Avoid cyclic dependencies between packages.*

Taking the packaging idea a stage further, some projects include an even higher level package structure for different levels of abstraction – Analysis Model, Design Model, and Implementation Model – and you can see this too in *Figure 27 Class Package Structure*.

The various UML diagrams may be more or less useful at the different levels of abstraction. In the Analysis Model, activity diagrams and use case diagrams may be predominant in describing business processes and specifying user requirements. In the Design Model, sequence diagrams and class diagrams may be predominant in documenting the realizations of use cases. In the Implementation Model, component diagrams may be predominate in demonstrating how the software solution will be decomposed into a set of deployable components.

Depending on the software development process you are following, you might use the same idea but with different names. For example: in an MSF project you might include Conceptual Design and Logical Design high level packages.

In some technology migration projects it is common to see a high level package structure comprising two packages: the *As-Is* model (representing the current system), and the *To-Be* model (representing the new enhanced system).

As an alternative to using higher level packages, you might consider creating separate *UML Modeling Projects* within a solution to represent the different levels of abstraction or for the *As-Is* and *To-Be* models.

Modeling and Validating the Architecture

Modeling and validating the architecture might naturally fall into this chapter on best practices; but since it is realized by new code-centric tools in Visual Studio 2010, I save the nuts-and-bolts detail until the next chapter: *Chapter 5 – Visual Studio 2010 UML for Developers*. Here I simply outline the new tools.

The list of diagram templates for a UML Modeling Project includes two additional diagram types whose names are not prefixed with 'UML': the Layer Diagram and the Directed Graph Document.

These diagrams allow you to:

a) Model the proposed architecture of your software solution as a set of interdependent layers, map your solution artifacts (classes or project assemblies) onto these layers, and validate this mapping against the real life code-level dependencies of your solution. This is the *Layer Diagram*.

b) Generate a visual schematic of the dependencies between your implemented classes, assemblies, or namespaces, as a handy cross-check against your conceptual UML class- and component- diagrams. This is the *Directed Graph Document*.

As stated before: since validating your architecture or generating a dependency graph for your code base requires a 'code base', I have included the nuts-and-bolts detail of these two diagram types in *Chapter 5 – Visual Studio 2010 UML for Developers*.

Architecture Explorer

Visual Studio 2010 Ultimate Edition also includes an *Architecture Explorer* that allows you to select vertical slices of code that you wish to visualize. You can drill down through your architecture, and run pre-defined and user-defined queries to explore architectural elements.

Again, I save the detail for the next chapter.

Software Development Processes

As stated in my definition in *Chapter 1 – UML, End-to-End*, UML is merely a *notation* and not a software development *process*. Successful software development depends on a good process.

Historically UML has been used predominantly in conjunction with the Rational Unified Process (RUP), but it need not be, and it is perfectly possible to use UML notation in conjunction with any software development process including the (nowadays) more popular 'agile' methods. In the context of .NET software development, the most logical choice of software development process may be the Microsoft Solutions Framework (MSF) process as enacted by the Team Foundation Server.

When utilizing some software development processes you will need to do a little translation between UML terminology and the terminology of the process. For example: where UML talks of *actors* and *use cases*, the MSF process talks of *personas* and *scenarios.*, and Agile methods talk of *user stories*.

Actors and Use Cases vs. Personas and Scenarios

The MSF concepts of personas and scenarios are very close to the Rational Unified Process (and hence UML) concepts of actors and use cases. The main distinctions are:

- Where an actor will have a generic role name, a persona will have a specific real name.

- Whereas a use case specification describes several possible interaction flows to achieve a functional goal, a scenario represents a single specific interaction flow.

Think of it like this:

"Jack" (the persona) is a *"Delivery Man"* (the actor) who *"takes out his van every morning at 08:00"* (the scenario) so as to *"Deliver an Order"* (the goal, or use case).

Another persona named *"John"* might also be a *"Delivery Man"* who *"takes out his van at 18:00 every evening"* so as to *"Deliver an Order"*. While the persona is different, the actor is the same; and while the scenario is different, the goal (or use case) is the same.

In some UML tools it would be possible to give each actor a *classifier name* and an *instance name*, so your use case diagram might show actors `Jack : Delivery Man` and `John : Delivery Man`. This appears not to be possible in Visual Studio 2010 UML, and in any case is probably overkill.

The best approach may be to keep use case diagrams simple and generic, and to include the extra details required for personas and scenarios in supporting documents (i.e. use case specifications) and *use case realization* sequence diagrams.

Remember that you can use an *Artifact* item from the *Use Case Diagram Toolbox* to hyperlink a use case specification document or web page to a use case. Remember also that you can use multiple sequence diagrams to represent the various use case 'scenario' paths, and – as shown in *Figure 11 Pick Stock Sequence Diagram* – you give the actors their persona names in these diagrams.

Microsoft Team Foundation Server

If you're running a non-trivial software development project in a Microsoft Visual Studio environment, there's a good chance you'll be using the Team Foundation Server to enact your software development process – whether it be RUP, MSF, or Agile.

You can find out more about the interaction between the Microsoft Visual Studio Team System and the Team Foundation Server in the book "Professional Visual Studio 2005 Team System" published by Wrox Press.

Two concepts are core to using the Team Foundation Server: *work items*, and *change control*.

Work Items

You can use the UML Model Explorer to link any UML model element with a work item. For example you might link a *User Story* work item to an *Activity Diagram*, or a *Test Case* work item to a *Use Case*, or a *Bug* work item to a specific *Operation* on a *Class*.

Just right-click any class, use case, diagram, component, operation, or pretty much anything else in the *UML Model Explorer* and choose *Link to Work Item* from the pop-up context menu.

Version Control

You can place your UML modeling projects and diagrams under Team Foundation Server *version control*, just as you would with code source files.

Since each *package* that you create is in effect a model-within-a-model with its own model definition (.uml) file, it is possible for two people to work on the same modeling project under version control providing you diligently decompose your model into packages.

In my running example, one user might work safely on classes and diagrams in the Accounts package while another user works on classes and diagrams in the Logistics package.

Complete coverage of Team Foundation Server Version Control is beyond the scope of this book, and I refer you to the book "Professional Team Foundation Server" published by Wrox.

Top-Down, Bottom-Up, and Iterative Modeling

The previous chapter focused on how a business analyst or software designer might use UML to model a business problem and its corresponding software solution in top-down fashion.

The next chapter focuses on how a software developer or architect might use UML and UML-like diagrams to visualize the code of an already-implemented solution.

In reality, your project is likely to encompass both approaches in an iterative process. Once the analysts and designers have documented the business problem and produced a 'first cut' solution, the architects and developers are likely to proceed by developing the code and the model side by side. The implementation model, and possibly the design model too, will be affected as the coded solution is refined; and it is important to ensure that the final model and the final code are representations of the same thing.

In this context you should consider in particular the difference between the UML Class Diagram discussed in the previous chapter and the DSL Class Designer discussed in the next chapter.

It is unlikely that the business problem will have changed in the course of developing the software solution, but it's not impossible.

It is also possible that your software development process will be incremental, with each additional increment providing additional vertical slice of functionality. Thus it is possible that the developers are implementing a particular use case subsystem while the analysts and designers are still modeling another subsystem.

In this context you should consider the division of use cases into subsystems discussed in the previous chapter, and the dependencies between class packages discussed in this chapter.

Summary

In this chapter you have been introduced to some best practices for extending UML using profiles, for structuring your UML models, and for using UML in the context of a software development process. The aim here has been to kick-start your further reading and research.

Having highlighted the distinction between top-down UML conceptual design, and bottom-up or iterative code development, in the next chapter we move from conceptual design modeling to code-level architectural design.

5 – Visual Studio 2010 UML for Developers

I'll admit up front that the title of this chapter is something of a misnomer. With the exception of *Sequence Diagrams*, the diagrams that I demonstrate here are not UML per-se. However, the *Class Designer* discussed herein is a UML-like diagram that serves the same purpose for the developer that the *UML Class Diagram* serves for the analyst or conceptual designer. And the other two diagrams – the *Layer Diagram* and the *Directed Graph Document* – are listed as templates alongside the five supported UML diagrams of a *UML Modeling Project*. So I have some justification for informally attaching a 'UML' label to this chapter. And where I refer to Developers, I mean this in the widest possible sense to also include Software Architects, or – to put it another way – anyone who works with code.

Class Designer

Whereas a business analyst or software designer is likely to utilize the new *Class Diagram* artifact in Visual Studio 2010 (or even use Visio) in order to perform top-down analysis and design, a developer may be more likely to utilize the *Class Designer* that was first introduced in Visual Studio 2005.

Class Designer provides a UML-like representation of the underlying code. Strictly speaking it's not UML notation, and so you cannot create a *Class Designer* class diagram in a UML modeling project. To create a diagram using *Class Designer* you must add a language-specific code project – for example a *Class Library*, *ASP.NET Web Application*, or *Windows Application* – to the solution as shown in *Figure 28 Add Visual C# Windows Forms Application*. To keep things simple I have chosen to add a *Visual C# Windows Forms Application*, but it could have been (for example) a Visual Basic ASP.NET Web Application.

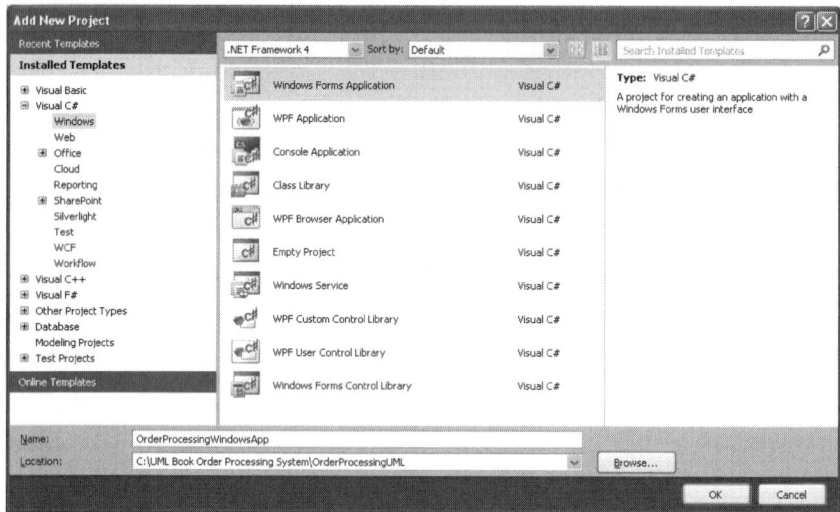

Figure 28 Add Visual C# Windows Forms Application

A code project is required because whereas a UML *Class Diagram* is a standalone design-time conceptual artifact, the *Class Designer* provides a class-diagram-like visual representation of *underlying code*. This means that the code and the visual representation are always in step – guaranteed – and there are none of the problems associated with traditional 'round trip engineering' between UML models and software code.

Another happy side-effect is that to draw Class Designer diagrams you do not need the Ultimate Edition of Visual Studio; which is a compelling argument in these days of tightening IT budgets.

Now that I have a code project I can add a *Class Designer* (not UML) class diagram to the project as shown in *Figure 29 Add Class Designer Class Diagram*. Notice how the file extension for this diagram is .cd whereas the UML class diagram created in *Chapter 3 – Visual Studio 2010 UML for Analysts and Designers* had file extension .classdiagram.

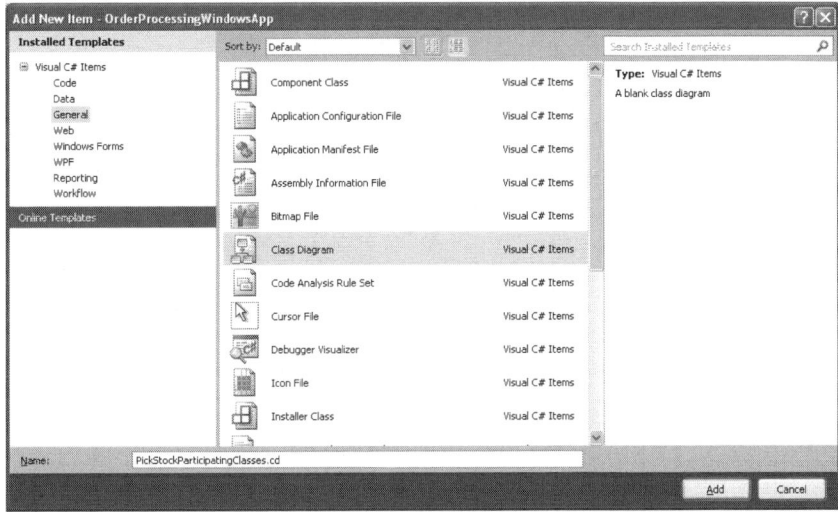

Figure 29 Add Class Designer Class Diagram

In this example I create pretty much the same class diagram as before so that you can compare the two results. It would be nice if I could shortcut the process by dragging my *analysis* or *design* classes from the *UML Explorer* onto this diagram so as to render them as code-backed classes; but at present this appears not to be possible.

Chapter 6 – Visualization and Modeling Feature Pack suggests one possible solution to this problem.

So I draw all of those classes again by dragging the required elements from the toolbox shown in *Figure 30 Class Designer Toolbox*. You can see that the toolbox items are similar to, but not exactly the same as, the items available in the *UML Class Diagram* toolbox (see *Figure 14 Class Diagram Toolbox*). From a coding point of view – in Visual C# at least – there is no distinction between *association*, *aggregation*, and *composition*, which all become object references in code. And, some language-specific code constructs – like *Delegate*, *Enum* and *Struct* – have no direct equivalent in UML. These differences distinguish the

Domain Specific Language (DSL) implemented by the *Class Designer* from the general purpose notation supported by UML.

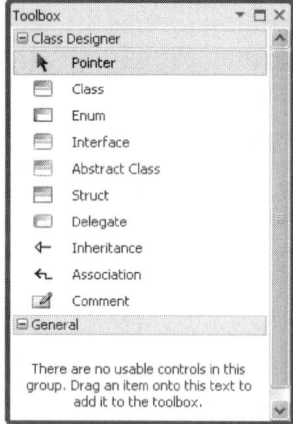

Figure 30 Class Designer Toolbox

Figure 31 Pick Stock Participating Classes in Class Designer shows my representation of the original Pick Stock 'Participating Classes' diagram (see *Figure 18 Pick Stock Participating Classes*) now drawn using *Class Designer*. It looks quite similar, but more informative than the similarities are the differences.

UML Software Design with Visual Studio 2010

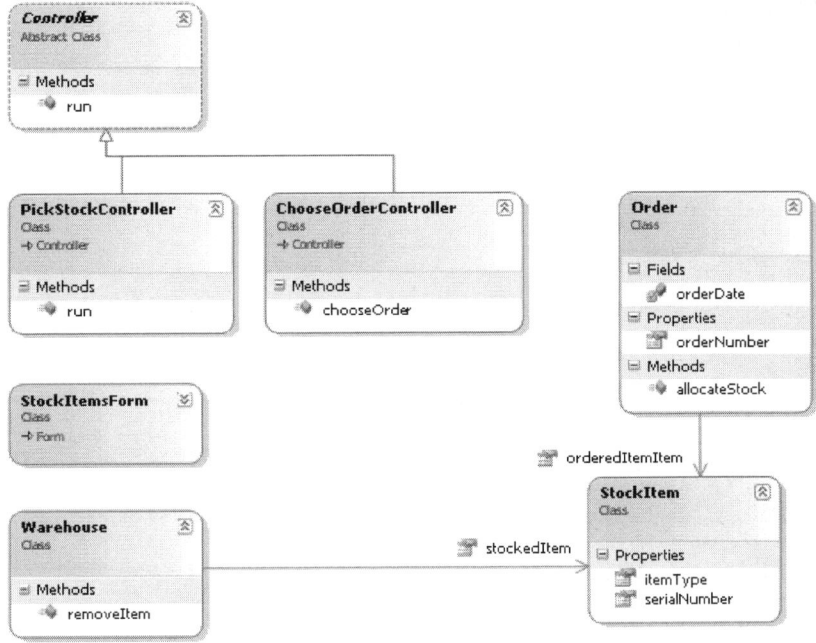

Figure 31 Pick Stock Participating Classes in Class Designer

The first difference you will notice is that none of the dependency links are shown, for example between ChooseOrderController and Order. This is because such dependencies are not implemented in code via object references.

The second difference you will notice is that what was formerly an aggregation relationship has now been modeled merely as an *Association*. This is because there is no distinction between association, aggregation and composition in Visual C# code – all of these being represented in code as a simple object reference.

The third difference you will notice is that one-to-many relationships are not indicated by a '*' or '1..*' indicator on association lines. I can fix this by altering the underlying code (double-click the class on the diagram) and changing the stockItem property from…

```
public StockItem stockedItem
```

to...

```
public List<StockItem> stockedItem
```

Once I've made this code change I can right-click the association on the diagram and choose *Show as Property* from the pop-up context menu; and then right-click the stockItem property and choose *Show as Collection Association* so as to render the association with a double fishtail as shown in *Figure 32 One-to-Many Association in Class Designer*.

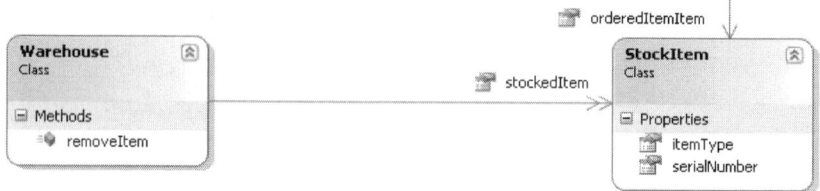

Figure 32 One-to-Many Association in Class Designer

So whereas UML would indicate a one-to-many relationship with a '*' or '1..*' annotation on an association line, the *Class Designer* uses this double fishtail representation.

Aside from the obvious significant differences between UML class diagrams and the *Class Designer*, just discussed, there are some other more subtle differences: like the fact that UML *Operations* are here referred to as *Methods*, and that UML *Attributes* can be represented as private *Fields* or public *Properties*.

The main selling point of the *Class Designer* compared with UML class diagrams is the 100% code synchronization. You have seen an example of this where I edited the underlying code of the stockItem property and saw the result of that change reflected in the diagram.

Whenever you add a new class to a *Class Designer* class diagram, a new skeleton class definition is created in your code base. And when you add a method, field or property to a class in *Class Designer*, the appropriate edit is made for you in the code… automatically. I have found this feature particularly useful when I am working in multiple .NET languages and I can't quite remember the syntax for specifying an inheritance relationship in C# code and compared with Visual Basic code. I just draw the inheritance relationship on the diagram, and the correct syntax is included in the code.

Reverse Engineering Sequence Diagrams

In the early days of UML modeling tools it always struck me that the tool vendors were missing a trick in allowing developers to reverse engineer *Static Structure Class Diagrams* from code, but not the dynamic UML diagrams such as *Sequence Diagrams* – despite sufficient information being deducible from the code.

How to Reverse Engineer a Sequence Diagram

On many of the projects that I engaged with, I solved the problem just highlighted by developing my own utilities to reverse engineer sequence diagrams. One way to do this would be to instrument the target application using code similar to that shown below; the purpose of which is to produce a trace of which objects invoke which operations on which other objects as the program runs.

```
public static void LogInvocation() // ** Trace method added by Tony Loton / LOTONtech
{
    // ** START INSTRUMENTATION **
    System.Diagnostics.StackTrace stackTrace=new System.Diagnostics.StackTrace();
    System.Diagnostics.StackFrame topFrame=stackTrace.GetFrame(1);
    System.Diagnostics.StackFrame nextFrame=stackTrace.GetFrame(2);
    String __callee=":";
    if (nextFrame!=null) __callee=":"+nextFrame.GetMethod().DeclaringType;
    System.Diagnostics.Trace.Write("<INVOCATION time="+DateTime.Now.ToString()+">");
```

```
System.Diagnostics.Trace.Write(__callee);

System.Diagnostics.Trace.Write("|"+topFrame.GetMethod());

System.Diagnostics.Trace.Write("|:"+topFrame.GetMethod().DeclaringType);

System.Diagnostics.Trace.WriteLine("</INVOCATION>");

    // ** END INSTRUMENTATION **

}
```

The application code would be modified, automatically or manually, so that every operation included the following statement as the first line:

```
TraceUtil.LogInvocation(); // ** INSTRUMENTATION added by Tony Loton / LOTONtech
```

There are other ways to trace the behavior of a running application in a less invasive way, but regardless of how it be done, the point would be to produce an output file with content similar to that given below:

```
<INVOCATION time=13/11/2003 11:26:44>:DSV._Default|Void
.ctor()|:DSV.DSVPage</INVOCATION>

<INVOCATION time=13/11/2003 11:26:46>:DSV.WebClassLibrary.AdminOperatorAccount|Void
.ctor()|:DSV.DSVManagement.BLL.CompanyManager</INVOCATION>

<INVOCATION time=13/11/2003
11:26:46>:DSV.WebClassLibrary.AdminOperatorAccount|DSV.Common.CompanyInfo
GetCompany(Char, Int32)|:DSV.DSVManagement.BLL.CompanyManager</INVOCATION>
```

The next step would be to devise a script or a *Visual Basic for Applications* (VBA) macro for a UML modeling tool such as *Rational Rose, Rational XDE,* or *Visio for Enterprise Architects*; the purpose of this script or macro being to build a sequence diagram dynamically in the tool from the information contained within the trace file.

This approach worked surprisingly well and could produce accurate representations of the runtime behavior of an application in the form of sequence diagrams. But it's not the only way.

The other way, which has been utilized in some UML tools prior to Visual Studio 2010, is to generate a sequence diagram by analyzing the static code – either by parsing the code text or by using the .NET code reflection features.

Which approach is better – dynamic reverse engineering or static reverse engineering – may be a matter for debate, and is something of a moot point considering that Visual 2010 takes the static approach. The main difference is that whereas static reverse engineering must consider all possible (conditional) code paths in one go, dynamic reverse engineering can produce different sequences for different usage patterns that exercise different paths through the code. In UML terms, it's the difference between producing sequence diagrams for specific *scenarios* (dynamic reverse engineering) rather than generic *use cases* (static reverse engineering).

Reverse Engineering in Visual Studio 2010

To reverse engineer a particular operation or method into a sequence diagram you simply need to right-click in the code window and choose *Generate Sequence Diagram* as shown in *Figure 33 Generate Sequence Diagram, Step 1*.

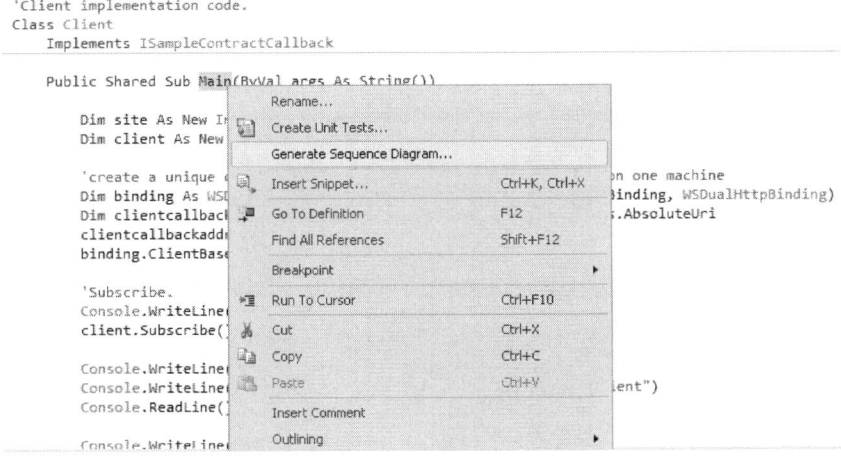

Figure 33 Generate Sequence Diagram, Step 1

Notice that you perform this reverse engineering on a method-by-method basis, rather than on a class-by-class basis, because a sequence diagram reflects an execution path; and therefore you need to specify an entry point to some execution.

In the next step, shown in *Figure 34 Generate Sequence Diagram, Step 2*, you choose a level of detail for the resultant sequence diagram.

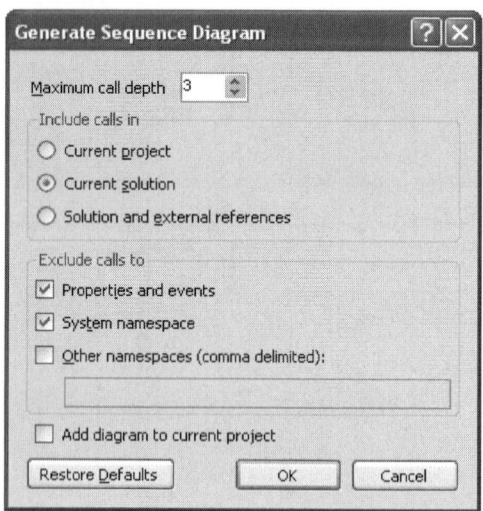

Figure 34 Generate Sequence Diagram, Step 2

When developing my own home-grown sequence diagram reverse engineering utilities, it didn't take long for something to dawn on me: whereas explicitly instrumented code results in a necessarily limited sequence diagram (limited to only those classes and methods that you instrument), when reverse engineering based on non-invasive runtime analysis or reflective code analysis you have to know where to stop.

Should your sequence diagram show only the essential interactions between the business objects in your business logic layer, or should it also show the invocations of objects in your data access layer; should it show interactions with (and between) classes in external class libraries and the core .NET system assemblies? And is it really meaningful to see interactions that are twenty levels deep when three levels would do just as well?

These are the questions you should ask yourself when checking the various boxes in the *Generate Sequence Diagram* dialog just shown.

It means the difference between *Figure 35 Less Detailed Sequence Diagram* and *Figure 36 More Detailed Sequence Diagram*. In the second diagram I have begun to scroll down, and I have shown the horizontal scroll bar on the diagram window, to give you an idea of the scale of this diagram compared with the first one.

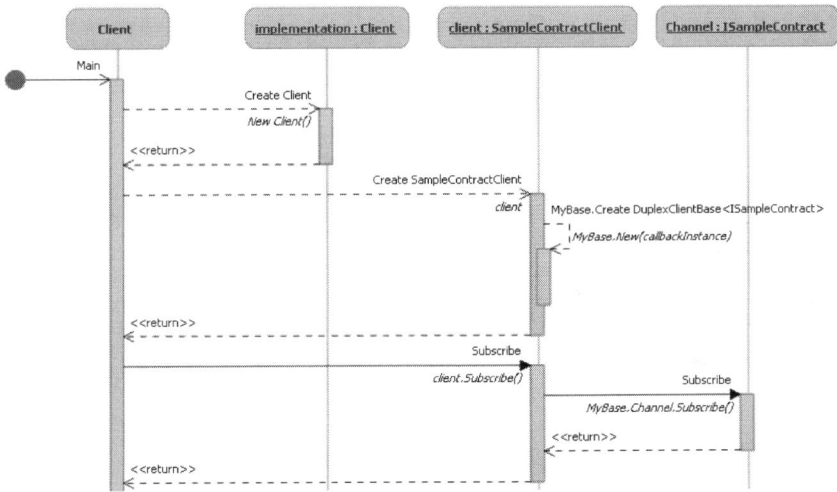

Figure 35 Less Detailed Sequence Diagram

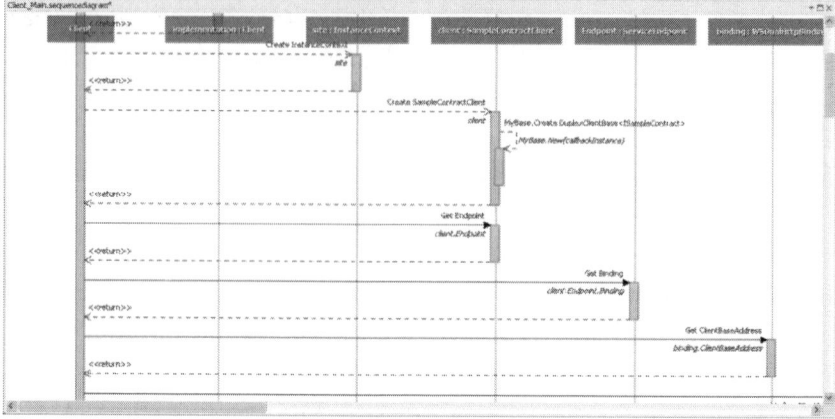

Figure 36 More Detailed Sequence Diagram

Note that while I have reverse engineered from one of the Visual Studio 2010 Visual Basic examples in here, this reverse engineering feature is not limited to Visual Basic.

Creating Layer Diagrams

If you look back at *Figure 3 Add a UML Diagram* in *Chapter 3 – Visual Studio 2010 UML for Analysts and Designers* you will see that among the UML diagrams that you can add to a modeling project there is also a *Layer Diagram*.

Since this diagram may not strictly be UML, I left it out of *Chapter 3 – Visual Studio 2010 UML for Analysts and Designers*. And since it is relevant to a project implemented in code, I include it here.

The toolbox for this diagram is shown in *Figure 37 Layer Diagram Toolbox*, and the toolbox items are:

Layer: represents an architectural layer of your software solution.

Dependency: shows that solution artifacts mapped onto one layer are dependent on solution artifacts mapped onto another layer.

Bidirectional Dependency: shows a mutual interdependence between solution artifacts in one layer and solution artifacts in another layer.

Comment: allows you to add descriptive text to the diagram.

Comment Link: allows you to link a comment to a specific diagram element.

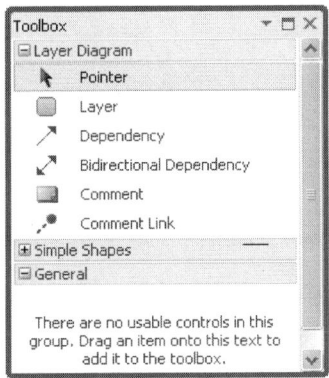

Figure 37 Layer Diagram Toolbox

Once you have drawn a set of layers, and colored them if you wish using the *Properties* window, you can drag *solution artifacts* onto the layers. Note that I said 'solution artifacts', and not 'UML artifacts'. This is more of a developer- or architect- level diagram onto which you can drag items from the *Solution Explorer* rather than from the *UML Model Explorer*.

Since my running example follows the Model-View-Controller pattern, in *Figure 38 Order Processing Layer Diagram* I have used a *Layer Diagram* to show the decomposition of my solution into a View layer, Controller layer, and a Model layer. Alternatively I might have named these layers the Presentation layer, the Web Services layer (if this were a web services implementation) and the Data layer.

By way of demonstration I have dragged two source files from *Solution Explorer* onto each of the layers, as appropriate, to show which implemented classes belong to which layer. Yes, it would be more logical to arrange the layers vertically in this diagram, but it saves space in this book to arrange them horizontally.

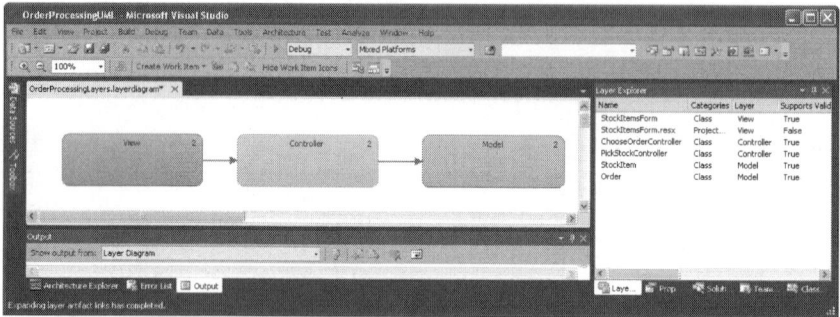

Figure 38 Order Processing Layer Diagram

The mappings are:

Name	Layer
StockItemsForm	View
ChooseOrderController	Controller
PickStockController	Controller
StockItem	Model
Order	Model

Validating the Architecture

The layer diagram is not just a pretty picture; it can serve a useful purpose in validating your architecture.

To demonstrate this, I introduce an architectural error by modifying the code for my StockItem class so that it includes a reference to the StockItemsForm, as follows:

```
public class StockItem
```

```
{
    public StockItemsForm theForm;
```

Cleary this modification would violate the architecture because a class in the Model layer should not be dependent on a class in the View layer.

So now let's run the validation.

In *Figure 39 Validate Architecture* you can see that I have right-clicked the layer diagram and chosen *Validate Architecture* from the context menu.

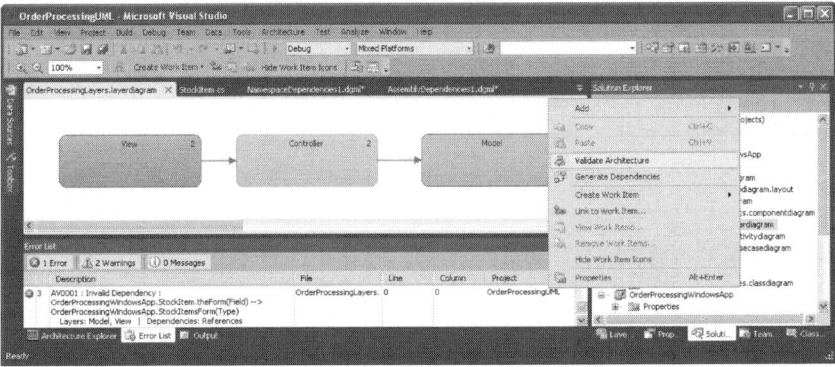

Figure 39 Validate Architecture

In the figure, you may or may not be able to see an error has been generated in the *Error List*. The error *Description* reads...

```
Error 3 AV0001 : Invalid Dependency :
OrderProcessingWindowsApp.StockItem.theForm(Field) -->
OrderProcessingWindowsApp.StockItemsForm(Type)
```

This is exactly the error I was expecting, and I could now go on to correct it either by modifying the code (to remove the offending reference) or by modifying the layer diagram to include a *Dependency* between the Model layer and the View layer. The second course of action would obviously be nonsensical since it would violate the Model-View-Controller design pattern, but it would be one way of resolving the error.

Having resolved the problem one way or another, a subsequent run of the *Validate Architecture* option would yield the following result in the *Output* window:

```
Architecture validation succeeded (0 suppressed).
```

Dependency Graphs / Directed Graph Documents

When adding a diagram to a modeling project you will notice a final diagram type called the *Directed Graph Document*. Again, it's not an official UML diagram.

It is possible to create a *Directed Graph Document* from existing artifacts; so in this spirit I select my OrderProcessingWindowsApp project in *Solution Explorer* and choose *By Class* from the *Generate Dependency Graph* item of the *Architecture* menu. The result is shown in *Figure 40 Class Dependencies Directed Graph Document*.

The diagram shows the dependencies between classes in my code base that result from one class inheriting from another class or from referencing another class. As such, this diagram serves as a useful cross-check against the conceptual *UML Class Diagram* that I created originally.

In the figure you can see that a dependency has been deduced between the ChooseOrderController and the Controller base class (and the same with the PickStockController) as you would expect, because each of these classes inherit from the Controller class. A dependency has been deduced between the Order class and StockItem class, because the Order class has a property of type StockItem. Note that, disappointingly, no dependency has been deduced between the Warehouse class and the StockItem class despite my code for the Warehouse class including the following property declaration:

```
public class Warehouse
    {
        public List<StockItem> stockedItem
```

So it seems that collection dependencies cannot be deduced automatically.

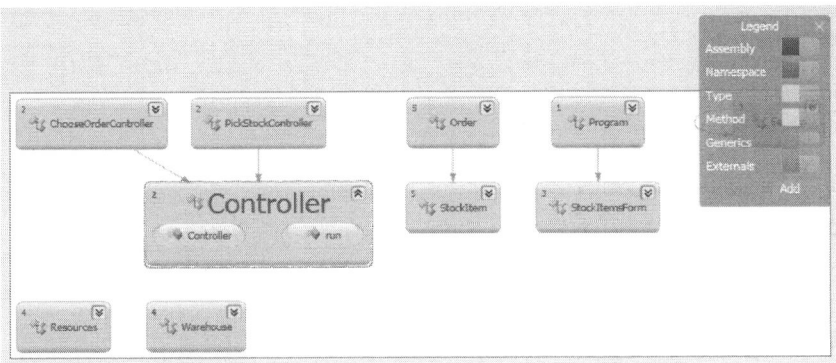

Figure 40 Class Dependencies Directed Graph Document

Whereas in this simple example I chose to generate dependencies between classes as a cross-check against my original UML class diagram(s), in a more complex solution it is also possible to generate dependencies between namespaces or between project assemblies (.exe files and .dll files) as a cross-check against your *UML Component Diagram*.

Analyzing Dependencies

As with the *Layer Diagram*, the *Directed Graph Document* is not just a pretty picture. It can be used, for example, to explore architectural aspects such as the degree of coupling between application tiers.

The trick to architecting a three-tier or client-server solution is to reduce the coupling between the client tier and the server (or service) tier. Client classes should interact with a limited number of server-side façade classes, which have well-defined interfaces and which hide the server-side complexity. Simply viewing the dependencies on the diagram can tell us a lot about the degree of coupling between classes or components, but there's more.

We can right-click the diagram surface and select one of the three *Analyzers* from the context menu as shown in *Figure 41 Analyzers / Unreferenced Nodes*. In this case I have run the analysis of *Unreferenced Nodes* (classes that are not referenced by any other class) in my partially-developed simple running example. For a more complex complete selection we might choose to analyze:

- *Circular References*: to find mutually-dependent classes that must be implemented in tandem.

- *Find Hubs*: so that we know which classes act as channels for messages between other classes, and which are therefore candidate façades in a client-server or multi-tier solution.

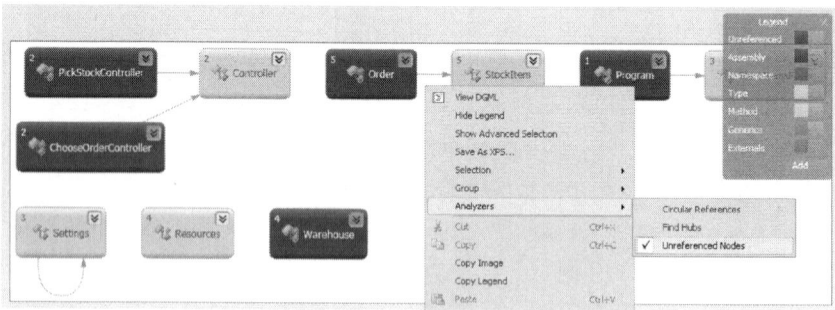

Figure 41 Analyzers / Unreferenced Nodes

Architecture Explorer

Using *Architecture Explorer* you can explore source code in a Visual Studio solution or compiled code. You are limited to exploring Visual C# .NET or Visual Basic .NET code unless you install the optional feature pack described in *Chapter 6 – Visualization and Modeling Feature Pack*.

You can access *Architecture Explorer* from the *Windows* item of the Visual Studio *Architecture* menu.

In *Figure 42 Architecture Explorer* you can see how I can use *Architecture Explorer* to drill down from a solution to individual projects, sources files, classes (and other types), and members. You can also see how I can select architectural elements for inclusion on a *Directed Graph Document* (by clicking one of the icons to the left).

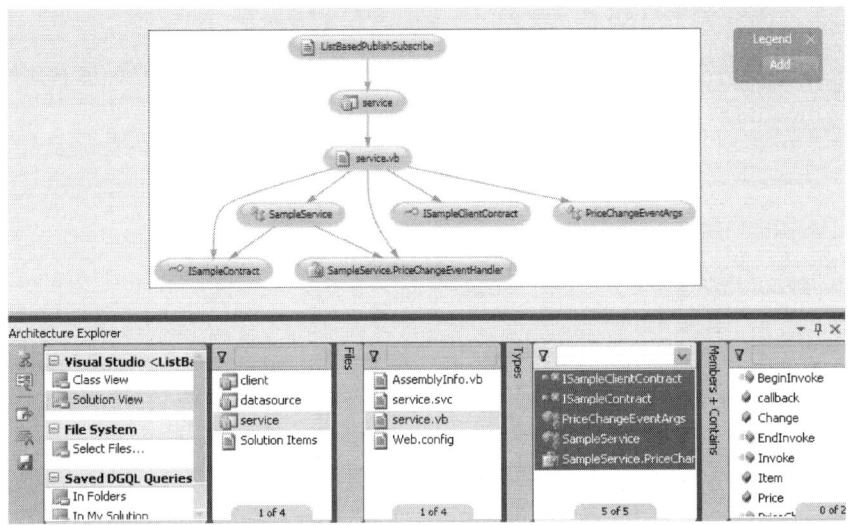

Figure 42 Architecture Explorer

In this example I have driven my architecture browsing session from the *Solution View*. I could otherwise have browsed via the *Class View*.

Note that at each architectural level it is possible to search and filter, so as to make the displayed results more manageable. For example, you might apply filters in order to display only *Enum* types, or all *constructor* methods. These may be saved as architecture 'queries' alongside the predefined Directed Graph Query Language (DGQL) queries that come with Visual Studio 2010. In *Figure 43 DGQL 'Public Classes' Query* you can see how I can access the predefined 'Public Classes' DGQL query.

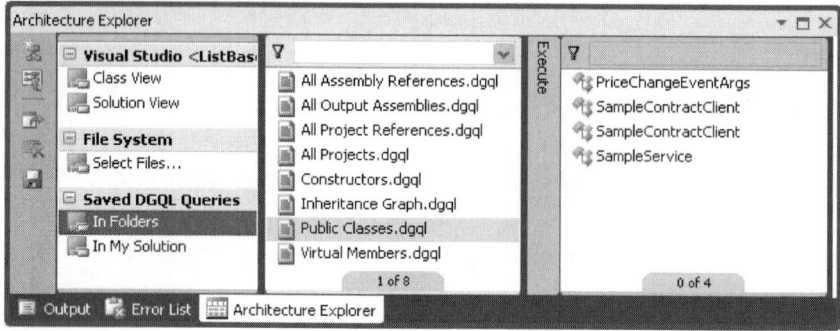

Figure 43 DGQL 'Public Classes' Query

Summary

In this chapter you have learnt about the more code-oriented UML and UML-like diagrams provided in the Visual Studio 2010 IDE; these being of particular interest to developers and software architects.

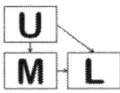

6 – Visualization and Modeling Feature Pack

The formal inclusion of UML within the Visual Studio 2010 IDE is good as far as it goes, and is long overdue. But it's not yet complete and is still lacking some of the interoperability features of other peer UML tools – such as the ability to round-trip from UML to code and back again, and the ability to import UML models from other tools.

These shortcomings are addressed (along with a few more additional features) by the Visualization and Modeling Feature Pack that is available to MSDN subscribers at http://msdn.microsoft.com/en-gb/vstudio/ff655021.aspx.

Complete coverage of the likely-to-change feature pack is beyond the scope of this book which covers the 'core' UML offerings of Visual Studio 2010 that are likely to remain static for some time (which in IT terms probably means about two years). However, I will share some of my thoughts on these feature pack additions.

Code Generation and Reverse Engineering

The ability to generate code stubs from a UML model is a necessary addition in the sense that other UML tools do it; and without this capability there would be no way to leverage fully the hard work done in conceptual analysis and design because – as I demonstrated in *Chapter 5 – Visual Studio 2010 UML for Developers* – you would have to re-draw all of your classes again using the code-centric *Class Designer*.

What I find curious is that after taking great pains to devise a *Domain Specific Language (DSL)* that assures 100% synchronization between the model and the code, so as to overcome the inevitable loss-in-translation of traditional UML code generation, Microsoft has now decided that the potential loss of fidelity may not be so bad after all.

This loss-in-translation has traditionally been made worse by attempting to generate code from the model, modifying the code, and then in a separate step reverse engineering the code back into the UML model; in the process known as round-trip engineering.

With the current toolset I would suggest the best approach to be for the software designer to generate code stubs initially from the UML model using Visual Studio 2010 Ultimate Edition plus the feature pack, and thereafter for the developer to use the *Class Designer* as a fully synchronized visual representation of the code in Visual Studio 2010 Professional.

Where the reverse engineering capability offered by the feature pack would be most useful (in my opinion) is in those all-too-prevalent situations where an existing code base has no formal design documentation and this is being demanded retrospectively. In this respect the revere engineering feature would be performing the same function as Visio 2010 Professional Edition as discussed in the next chapter.

At the time of writing, the code generation and reverse engineering features are limited to C# code; but the whole thing is based around the idea of extensible *transformations*. Those of you who are willing to dig deep enough can find out about creating your own transformations for other programming languages – or to generate other kinds of artifacts from UML models, not limited to code stubs.

XMI Import

XMI, which stands for XML Metadata Interchange, is the official Object Management Group (OMG) specification for exchanging model information between modeling tools and repositories.

In theory, XMI provides a lingua franca for porting your UML model from one visual modeling tool to another one. It may be useful if you've been working on a UML model using a tool such as Enterprise Architect (http://www.sparxsystems.com.au/) or Magic Draw (http://www.magicdraw.com/), and you now want to bring it into Visual Studio 2010.

You can't go the other way, because neither Visual Studio 2010 nor the feature pack (at the time of writing) support XMI export.

The XMI import feature currently supports XMI 2.1 import, with some obvious exceptions. Since Visual Studio 2010 does not support the complete set of UML diagrams, elements relating to state-chart diagrams and deployment diagrams will not be imported.

Exploring C and C++ Code in Architecture Explorer

As I mentioned in the previous chapter, the Visual Studio 2010 *Architecture Explorer* is limited to exploring Visual C# .NET and Visual Basic .NET code unless you have this feature pack installed; in which case you can also explore C / C++ code that includes *Unions*, *Typedefs* and *Members*.

Summary

In this chapter you have been introduced to the optional *Visualization and Modeling Feature Pack* that extends the UML capabilities of Visual Studio 2010 and which is available to MSDN subscribers.

UML Software Design with Visual Studio 2010

7 – Visio 2010 UML

In my earlier co-authored book *Professional UML with Visual Studio .NET : Unmasking Visio for Enterprise Architects* I showed how the UML diagramming features provided by Visio could be utilized in the up-front design and after-the-fact documenting of .NET applications that have been developed using Visual Studio.

With UML diagramming facilities now being provided within the Visual Studio IDE itself, you may wonder whether there is still a role for Visio in UML software development for .NET. Well, you might conclude that *there is* if you consider the following points:

- Software analysts and designers can use Visio Professional 2010 to draw conceptual UML diagrams without having access to – or being licensed for – Visual Studio 2010 Ultimate Edition.

- Developers can reverse engineer their code classes into a Visio UML model from Visual Studio 2010 Professional Edition; so again there may be no need for the Visual Studio 2010 Ultimate Edition when documenting an existing system in UML retrospectively.

In a nutshell: for some people, Visio Professional 2010 will provide an adequate and less costly option for their UML modeling needs. I have worked with at least one company recently (mid-2010) for whom this was the case.

Tony Loton

Top-Down Software Design

Since the focus of this book is the new set of UML features provided natively within the Visual Studio 2010 IDE, I do not intend to replicate the detailed guidance that was given in my earlier book regarding the top-down design of software systems in UML design using Visio.

The earlier book is still in print, and it should be sufficient here for me to say that in the latest Visio Professional 2010 you can still draw the full range of UML diagrams that you will find in this book and that you could draw using the earlier Visio versions.

Code Generation

Earlier versions of Visio, and in particular the Visio for Enterprise Architects version that shipped alongside Visual Studio .NET in 2003, allowed you to forward engineer from Visio UML classes into .NET code.

As far as I know, this ability has been deprecated such that it is no longer possible to generate the code stubs for .NET classes from a Visio model. The role of Visio is therefore limited to conceptual analysis and design; except that it is still possible to reverse engineer from a .NET solution into a Visio UML model as discussed next.

Reverse Engineering

While it is commonly accepted that we should design an application before coding it, there may be situations where we prefer to prototype an idea in code before designing it formally. Alternatively, we might be interfacing with another team or third-party supplier that is not disciplined enough to have produced a complete UML design model before cutting the code. We might even be members of that team, and now we must document our creation for handover to someone else.

Or, we might even have simply inherited a load of source code from the guy who has now left the company.

In these situations – all of which I have encountered in real life – it is useful to be able to model retrospectively an existing coded application using the Unified Modeling Language. In order to achieve this, we must convert the coded object classes into their UML class representations using the process known as a *reverse engineering*.

Reverse Engineering into Visio 2010

Initiate the reverse engineering process by first selecting a class, a project, or a whole solution in the *Solution Designer* of Visual Studio 2010; and then choose *Reverse Engineer* from the *Visio UML* item of the *Project* menu as shown in *Figure 44 Visio UML, Reverse Engineer*. If this menu option does not appear, do check that you have Visio 2010 installed rather than an earlier version.

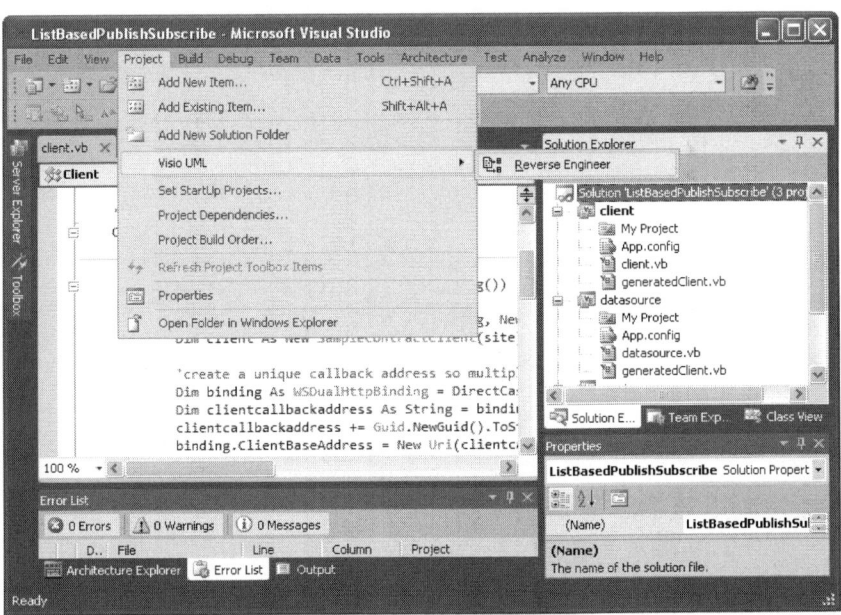

Figure 44 Visio UML, Reverse Engineer

A dialog will appear, asking you to *Select Visio UML File*; which at this point of course won't exist, so you'll accept the suggested name of the new file. In my example the new Visio file would be called ListBasedPublishSubscribe.vsd, mirroring the name of the solution I'm reverse engineering in this example, and it would be added to the *Solution Items* shown in *Solution Explorer*.

In *Figure 45 Reverse Engineered Code Classes in Visio* you can see that the *Visio Model Explorer* contains a *Static Model* with a folder structure mirroring that of the original Visual Studio solution.

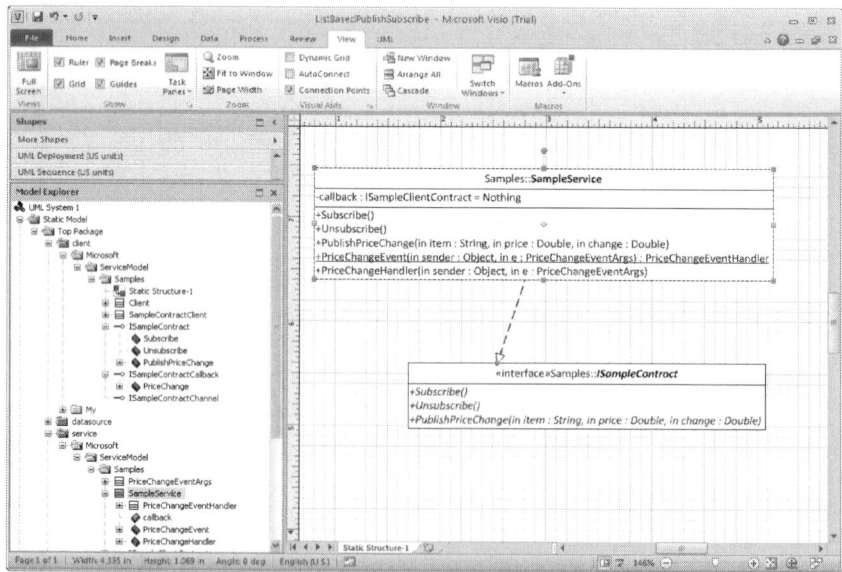

Figure 45 Reverse Engineered Code Classes in Visio

You can also see that I have dragged one of the classes and one of the interfaces from the *Model Explorer* onto the Visio canvas. This shows that the reverse engineering process has picked up the operations of each class, as well as the UML *generalization* or *implements* relationship between the ISampleContract interface and the SampleService class.

UML Software Design with Visual Studio 2010

Reverse Engineering, No Source Code Required

The kind of reverse engineering just described is fine if you have the source code for the .NET assembly that you'd like to represent using UML in Visio. But what if you don't? Wouldn't it be nice to be able to select a referenced assembly in the *Visual Studio Solution Explorer* and reverse engineer it into Visio? It seems that you can't.

Note that where one of the classes in your solution references a class in another assembly, for example by inheriting from a base class in a referenced assembly, the referenced class (in this case the base class) from the assembly will be reverse engineered into Visio.

In 2003 I devised the RE.NET (Reverse Engineering .NET) utility as an aid to reverse engineering *any* .NET assembly into a Visio UML model, no source code required.

The test drive that follows shows how this utility was used.

RE.NET Test Drive

I open a *Visual Studio Command Prompt* so that the environment path is set correctly, and then I type the following on the command line:

```
ReverseEngineer -v System.Data > System.Data.cs
```

In this case I have decided to reverse engineer the core .NET System.Data assembly, but it could be any third party .NET assembly DLL that I have placed in the current directory.

The result of my specified command line is a new file named System.Data.cs, which is a C# source code representation of the classes contained in the original assembly.

Now that I have source code stubs for the classes in the assembly, I can reverse engineer these into Visio in the usual way. So as an example, I create a new *Class Library* project in Visual Studio 2010 named ReverseEngineeredCode and I add the `System.Data.cs` file to it as shown in *Figure 46 Reverse Engineered Code Visual Studio Solution*. I then choose *Reverse Engineer* from the *Visio UML* option of the *Project* menu in Visual Studio.

You can see in the figure that I have already done this; therefore the solution contains a file named ReverseEngineeredCode.vsd.

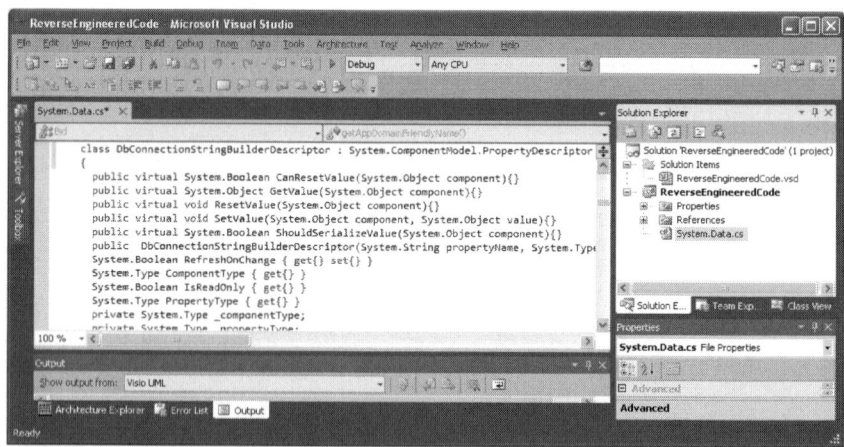

Figure 46 Reverse Engineered Code Visual Studio Solution

If you'd like to try your hand at this, and possibly take it further, or simply learn more about .NET reflection that drives the utility, you should find the source code for the RE.NET Reverse Engineering utility at www.lotontech.com/uml. It is also listed in *Appendix A – RE.NET Reverse Engineering C# Code* of this book.

Note that although I provide this utility for educational purposes, *you are responsible for complying with any license terms regarding the reverse engineering of third party code.*

UML Software Design with Visual Studio 2010

Summary

This chapter has focused on the UML features retained in Visio Professional 2010, which for some UML practitioners will serve as an acceptable alternative to the native UML features of Visual Studio 2010 Ultimate Edition.

UML Software Design with Visual Studio 2010

Appendix A – RE.NET Reverse Engineering C# Code

The RE.NET (Reverse Engineer .NET) utility allows you to reverse engineer any .NET assembly DLL* – into source code stubs, and ultimately onto a Visio Static Structure Class Diagram – even if you don't have the original source code for the assembly. The assembly might be a third-party class library or one of the core .NET system libraries such as System.Data.

note that YOU are responsible for compliance with any restrictions regarding the reverse engineering of third party software.

Instructions for building and running the RE.NET utility are as follows:

Step 1 – Create Visual Studio Project

Create a new *Visual C# Console Application* project in Visual Studio, and name it ReverseEngineer. Add a new C# source file named ReverseEngineer.cs and paste the code shown at the foot of this page.

Step 2 – Build and Locate the Executable File

Build the project and locate the executable file ReverseEngineer.exe in the project /bin directory.

Step 3 – Run the Utility

Open a *Visual Studio Command Prompt* (so that the environment path is set correctly) and execute the ReverseEngineer application against your chosen DLL, like this:

```
ReverseEngineer -v System.Data > System.Data.cs
```

It doesn't need to be a .NET system assembly DLL that you reverse engineer, and you might just as well reverse engineer a third party assembly DLL – let's assume it's SuperThirdPartyGraphicsLibrary.dll – like this:

```
ReverseEngineer -v SuperThirdPartyGraphicsLibrary > SuperThirdPartyGraphicsLibrary.cs
```

Step 4 – Add Results to a new Class Library Project

Create a new *Visual C# Class Library* project in Visual Studio and add the file System.Data.cs or SuperThirdPartyGraphicsLibrary.cs from the previous step.

Step 5 – Reverse Engineer the Source Code Class Stubs

Select the source file in the Visual Studio *Solution Explorer* and choose *Reverse Engineer* from the *Visio UML* option of the Visual Studio *Project* menu. You can now create Static Structure Class Diagrams in Visio using the class definitions that have been imported.

ReverseEngineer.cs Reverse Engineering Source Code

In order to follow the preceding steps you will need the original source code for the RE.NET utility, which is listed warts 'n' all (I've not changed it) below. You should also be able to copy and paste it from my companion web site at www.lotontech.com/uml.

```csharp
using System;
using System.Reflection;
using System.Data;
using System.Text.RegularExpressions;

namespace reverse
{
    // ** RE.NET Assembly Reverse Engineering
    // ** by Tony Loton of LOTONtech Limited
    // ** www.lotontech.com/visualmodeling
    // **
    // ** You are free to copy, distribute, and use
    // ** this code as you wish, providing you retain
    // ** this comment.
    // **
    public class ReverseEngineer
    {
        private static bool roseFlag=false;
        private static bool visioFlag=false;
```

UML Software Design with Visual Studio 2010

```
        private static String currentClass="";
        private static DataTable assemblyTable=null;

        public static void Main(string[] args)
        {
            DataColumn[] keys = new DataColumn[7];

            // -- Build the table to hold the source model ---
            assemblyTable=new DataTable();

            // - sort class --
            DataColumn newColumn = new DataColumn();
            newColumn.DataType = System.Type.GetType("System.String");
            newColumn.AllowDBNull = false;
            newColumn.Caption = "sortclass";
            newColumn.ColumnName = "sortclass";
            assemblyTable.Columns.Add(newColumn);
            keys[0]=newColumn; // Add to primary key

            // - line num (within sort class) -
            newColumn = new DataColumn();
            newColumn.DataType = System.Type.GetType("System.Int32");
            newColumn.AllowDBNull = false;
            newColumn.Caption = "line";
            newColumn.ColumnName = "line";
            assemblyTable.Columns.Add(newColumn);

            // - two character metatype -
            newColumn = new DataColumn();
            newColumn.DataType = System.Type.GetType("System.String");
            newColumn.AllowDBNull = false;
            newColumn.Caption = "metatype";
            newColumn.ColumnName = "metatype";
            assemblyTable.Columns.Add(newColumn);
            keys[1]=newColumn; // Add to primary key

            // - visibility -
            newColumn = new DataColumn();
            newColumn.DataType = System.Type.GetType("System.String");
            newColumn.AllowDBNull = false;
            newColumn.Caption = "visibility";
            newColumn.ColumnName = "visibility";
            assemblyTable.Columns.Add(newColumn);
            keys[2]=newColumn; // Add to primary key

            // - static -
            newColumn = new DataColumn();
            newColumn.DataType = System.Type.GetType("System.String");
            newColumn.AllowDBNull = false;
            newColumn.Caption = "static";
            newColumn.ColumnName = "static";
            assemblyTable.Columns.Add(newColumn);
            keys[3]=newColumn; // Add to primary key

            // - abstract -
            newColumn = new DataColumn();
            newColumn.DataType = System.Type.GetType("System.String");
            newColumn.AllowDBNull = false;
            newColumn.Caption = "abstract";
            newColumn.ColumnName = "abstract";
            assemblyTable.Columns.Add(newColumn);
            keys[4]=newColumn; // Add to primary key

            // - name -
            newColumn = new DataColumn();
            newColumn.DataType = System.Type.GetType("System.String");
            newColumn.AllowDBNull = false;
            newColumn.Caption = "name";
            newColumn.ColumnName = "name";
            assemblyTable.Columns.Add(newColumn);
            keys[5]=newColumn; // Add to primary key

            // - type -
            newColumn = new DataColumn();
            newColumn.DataType = System.Type.GetType("System.String");
            newColumn.AllowDBNull = false;
            newColumn.Caption = "type";
            newColumn.ColumnName = "type";
            assemblyTable.Columns.Add(newColumn);
            keys[6]=newColumn; // Add to primary key

            // - virtual -
            newColumn = new DataColumn();
            newColumn.DataType = System.Type.GetType("System.String");
            newColumn.AllowDBNull = false;
            newColumn.Caption = "virtual";
            newColumn.ColumnName = "virtual";
            assemblyTable.Columns.Add(newColumn);
            //keys[7]=newColumn; // Add to primary key

            // - final -
            newColumn = new DataColumn();
            newColumn.DataType = System.Type.GetType("System.String");
```

```csharp
newColumn.AllowDBNull = false;
newColumn.Caption = "final";
newColumn.ColumnName = "final";
assemblyTable.Columns.Add(newColumn);
//keys[8]=newColumn; // Add to primary key

// -- Set primary key to (almost) all columns to ensure uniqueness --
assemblyTable.PrimaryKey=keys;

foreach (string assemblyName in args)
{
    if (assemblyName.Equals("-r") || assemblyName.Equals("-R"))
    {
        roseFlag=true;
        continue;
    }
    if (assemblyName.Equals("-v") || assemblyName.Equals("-V"))
    {
        visioFlag=true;
        continue;
    }

    Assembly sourceAssembly=Assembly.LoadWithPartialName(assemblyName);

    if (sourceAssembly==null) return;

    Type[] types=sourceAssembly.GetTypes();

    foreach (Type thisType in types)
    {
        processType(thisType);
    }
}

assemblyTable.AcceptChanges();

printSource(assemblyTable);
}

public static void processType(Type thisType)
{
    if (thisType.Name.Equals("AssemblyRef") || thisType.Name.Equals("ExternDll") || thisType.Name.Equals("ThisAssembly")) return;
    string visibility=" ";
    string staticFlag=" ";
    string abstractFlag=" ";
    string finalFlag=" ";
    string virtualFlag=" ";

    if (thisType.IsInterface)
    {
        if (thisType.IsPublic) visibility="+";
        else visibility=" ";

        currentClass=""+thisType;
                DataRow thisRow=assemblyTable.NewRow();
                thisRow["sortclass"]=currentClass;
        thisRow["line"]=0;
        thisRow["metatype"]="IN";
                thisRow["visibility"]=visibility;
                thisRow["static"]=staticFlag;
                thisRow["abstract"]=abstractFlag;
                thisRow["name"]=""+thisType;
                thisRow["final"]=finalFlag;
                thisRow["virtual"]=virtualFlag;
                thisRow["type"]="";

                try { assemblyTable.Rows.Add(thisRow); }
        catch (System.Data.ConstraintException) {}

        // -- Any implemented interfaces --
        int line=2;
        Type[] interfaces = thisType.GetInterfaces();
        foreach (Type thisInterface in interfaces)
        {
                    DataRow interfaceRow=assemblyTable.NewRow();
                    interfaceRow["sortclass"]=currentClass;
            interfaceRow["line"]=line++;
            interfaceRow["metatype"]="IM";
                    interfaceRow["visibility"]=" ";
                    interfaceRow["static"]=" ";
                    interfaceRow["abstract"]=" ";
                    interfaceRow["name"]=""+thisInterface;
                    interfaceRow["type"]="";
                    interfaceRow["virtual"]=" ";
                    interfaceRow["final"]=" ";
                    try { assemblyTable.Rows.Add(interfaceRow); }
            catch (System.Data.ConstraintException) {}
        }

                // -- The members --
                listMembers(thisType,line);
```

```
            }
            else if (thisType.IsClass)
            {
                if (thisType.IsAbstract) abstractFlag="@";

                if (thisType.IsPublic) visibility="+";
                else visibility=" ";

                // -- The class itself --

                currentClass=""+thisType;
                DataRow classRow=assemblyTable.NewRow();
                classRow["sortclass"]=currentClass;
                classRow["line"]=0;

                classRow["metatype"]="CL";

                classRow["visibility"]=visibility;
                classRow["static"]=staticFlag;
                classRow["abstract"]=abstractFlag;
                classRow["name"]=""+thisType;
                classRow["type"]="";
                classRow["final"]=finalFlag;
                classRow["virtual"]=virtualFlag;

                try { assemblyTable.Rows.Add(classRow); }
                catch (System.Data.ConstraintException) {}

                // -- Any superclass --

                DataRow superRow=assemblyTable.NewRow();
                superRow["sortclass"]=currentClass;
                superRow["line"]=1;
                superRow["metatype"]="SC";
                superRow["visibility"]=" ";
                superRow["static"]=" ";
                superRow["abstract"]=" ";
                superRow["name"]=""+thisType.BaseType;
                superRow["type"]="";
                superRow["virtual"]=" ";
                superRow["final"]=" ";
                try { assemblyTable.Rows.Add(superRow); }
                catch (System.Data.ConstraintException) {}

                // -- Any implemented interfaces --
                int line=3;
                Type[] interfaces = thisType.GetInterfaces();
                foreach (Type thisInterface in interfaces)
                {
                        DataRow interfaceRow=assemblyTable.NewRow();
                        interfaceRow["sortclass"]=currentClass;
                    interfaceRow["line"]=line++;
                    interfaceRow["metatype"]="IM";
                        interfaceRow["visibility"]=" ";
                        interfaceRow["static"]=" ";
                        interfaceRow["abstract"]=" ";
                        interfaceRow["name"]=""+thisInterface;
                        interfaceRow["type"]="";
                        interfaceRow["virtual"]=" ";
                        interfaceRow["final"]=" ";
                        try { assemblyTable.Rows.Add(interfaceRow); }
                    catch (System.Data.ConstraintException) {}
                }

                // -- The members --
                listMembers(thisType,line);
            }
    }

    public static void listMembers(Type thisType, int line)
    {
        MemberInfo[] members=thisType.GetMembers(BindingFlags.Public
                                        | BindingFlags.NonPublic
                                        | BindingFlags.Static
                                        | BindingFlags.Instance);

        foreach (MemberInfo thisMember in members)
        {
            // *** Is it defined on this class, i.e. not from a superclass? ***
            // *** Note that only public methods will be reflected ***
            if (thisMember.DeclaringType==thisMember.ReflectedType)
            {
                string visibility=" ";
                string staticFlag=" ";
                string abstractFlag=" ";
                string virtualFlag=" ";
                string finalFlag=" ";

                switch (""+thisMember.MemberType)
                {
                    case "NestedType":
                    {
                        Type typeInfo=(Type) thisMember;
```

```
                            visibility="-";

                                DataRow fieldRow=assemblyTable.NewRow();
                                    fieldRow["sortclass"]=currentClass;
                                fieldRow["line"]=line++;
                                fieldRow["metatype"]="NC";
                                        fieldRow["visibility"]=visibility;
                                        fieldRow["static"]=staticFlag;
                                        fieldRow["abstract"]=abstractFlag;

                            if (thisType.Namespace!=null)
fieldRow["name"]=thisType.Namespace+"."+thisMember.Name;
                            else fieldRow["name"]=thisMember.Name;

                                        fieldRow["type"]="";
                                        fieldRow["virtual"]=" ";
                                        fieldRow["final"]=" ";
                                        try { assemblyTable.Rows.Add(fieldRow); }
                                catch (System.Data.ConstraintException) {}

                            break;

                        }

                        case "Constructor":
                        {
                            ConstructorInfo constructorInfo=(ConstructorInfo) thisMember;

                            if (constructorInfo.IsAbstract && !thisType.IsInterface) abstractFlag="@";

                            // -- Ignore these flags for constructors --
                            // if (constructorInfo.IsStatic) staticFlag="$";
                            // if (constructorInfo.IsVirtual && !thisType.IsInterface) virtualFlag="v";
                            // if (constructorInfo.IsFinal) finalFlag="f";
                            // if (constructorInfo.IsPublic && !thisType.IsInterface) visibility="+";
                            // if (constructorInfo.IsPrivate) visibility="-";

                            // override constructor visibility to always be public?
                            visibility="+";

                            String signature="(";
                            ParameterInfo[] parameters=constructorInfo.GetParameters();
                            bool firstParam=true;
                            int pNum=0;
                            foreach (ParameterInfo parameterInfo in parameters)
                            {
                                if (!parameterInfo.IsRetval)
                                {
                                    String paramName=parameterInfo.Name;
                                    if (paramName==null)
                                    {
                                        paramName="p"+pNum;
                                        pNum++;
                                    }

                                    String paramType=""+parameterInfo.ParameterType;
                                    paramType=Regex.Replace(paramType,@"&","");

                                    if (!firstParam)
                                       signature=signature+", ";

                                    firstParam=false;

                                    signature=signature+paramType+" "+paramName;
                                }
                            }
                            signature=signature+")";
//                            String signature=""+constructorInfo;
//                            int bracketPos=signature.IndexOf("(");
//                            signature
//                               =signature.Substring(bracketPos,signature.Length-bracketPos);

                            // -- Remove any ByRef indicators --
                            signature=Regex.Replace(signature,@"\sByRef(\)|,)",",");
                            signature=Regex.Replace(signature,@",\s\.{3}",",");

                            DataRow methodRow=assemblyTable.NewRow();
                            methodRow["sortclass"]=currentClass;
                            methodRow["line"]=line++;
                            methodRow["metatype"]="CO";
                            methodRow["visibility"]=visibility;
                            methodRow["static"]=staticFlag;
                            methodRow["abstract"]=abstractFlag;
                            methodRow["virtual"]=virtualFlag;
                            methodRow["final"]=finalFlag;
                            methodRow["name"]=thisType.Name+signature;
                            methodRow["type"]=thisType.Name;

                            try { assemblyTable.Rows.Add(methodRow); }
                            catch (System.Data.ConstraintException) {}

                            break;
```

```csharp
            }
            case "Method":
            {
                MethodInfo methodInfo=(MethodInfo) thisMember;
                if (methodInfo.IsAbstract && !thisType.IsInterface) abstractFlag="@";
                if (methodInfo.IsStatic) staticFlag="$";
                if (methodInfo.IsVirtual && !thisType.IsInterface) virtualFlag="v";
                if (methodInfo.IsFinal) finalFlag="f";

                if (methodInfo.IsPublic && !thisType.IsInterface) visibility="+";
                else if (methodInfo.IsPrivate) visibility="-";
                else visibility="#";

                String signature="(";
                ParameterInfo[] parameters=methodInfo.GetParameters();
                bool firstParam=true;
                int pNum=0;
                foreach (ParameterInfo parameterInfo in parameters)
                {
                    if (!parameterInfo.IsRetval)
                    {
                        String paramName=parameterInfo.Name;
                        if (paramName==null)
                        {
                            paramName="p"+pNum;
                            pNum++;
                        }

                        String paramType=""+parameterInfo.ParameterType;
                        paramType=Regex.Replace(paramType,@"&","");

                        if (!firstParam)
                           signature=signature+", ";

                        firstParam=false;

                        signature=signature+paramType+" "+paramName;
                    }
                }
                signature=signature+")";
//                String signature=""+methodInfo;
//                int bracketPos=signature.IndexOf("(");
//                signature
//                   =signature.Substring(bracketPos,signature.Length-bracketPos);

//                // -- Remove any ByRef indicators --
//                signature=Regex.Replace(signature,@"\sByRef(\)|,)",",");
//                signature=Regex.Replace(signature,@",\s\.{3}",",");

                DataRow methodRow=assemblyTable.NewRow();
                methodRow["sortclass"]=currentClass;
                methodRow["line"]=line++;
                methodRow["metatype"]="ME";
                methodRow["visibility"]=visibility;
                methodRow["static"]=staticFlag;
                methodRow["abstract"]=abstractFlag;
                methodRow["virtual"]=virtualFlag;
                methodRow["final"]=finalFlag;
                methodRow["name"]=methodInfo.Name+signature;
                methodRow["type"]=methodInfo.ReturnType;

                // Only add the method if the name does not contain dots.
                if (methodInfo.Name.IndexOf(".")<0)
                {
                    try { assemblyTable.Rows.Add(methodRow); }
                    catch (System.Data.ConstraintException) {}
                }

                break;
            }
            case "Field":
            {
                FieldInfo fieldInfo=(FieldInfo) thisMember;

                if (fieldInfo.IsPublic) visibility="+";
                else if (fieldInfo.IsPrivate) visibility="-";
                else visibility="#";

                if (fieldInfo.IsStatic) staticFlag="$";

                        DataRow fieldRow=assemblyTable.NewRow();
                        fieldRow["sortclass"]=currentClass;
                fieldRow["line"]=line++;
                fieldRow["metatype"]="FI";
                        fieldRow["visibility"]=visibility;
                        fieldRow["static"]=staticFlag;
                        fieldRow["abstract"]=abstractFlag;
                        fieldRow["name"]=thisMember.Name;
                        fieldRow["type"]=fieldInfo.FieldType;
                        fieldRow["virtual"]=" ";
                        fieldRow["final"]=" ";
                        try { assemblyTable.Rows.Add(fieldRow); }
```

```
                    catch (System.Data.ConstraintException) {}

                    break;
                }
                case "Property":
                {
                    PropertyInfo propertyInfo=(PropertyInfo)thisMember;

                            DataRow propertyRow=assemblyTable.NewRow();
                            propertyRow["sortclass"]=currentClass;
                    propertyRow["line"]=line++;
                    propertyRow["metatype"]="PR";
                            propertyRow["visibility"]=visibility;
                            propertyRow["static"]=staticFlag;
                            propertyRow["abstract"]=abstractFlag;
                            propertyRow["name"]=thisMember.Name;
                            propertyRow["type"]=propertyInfo.PropertyType;
                            propertyRow["virtual"]=" ";

                    // *** Only for properties, this flag is used to determine if
                    // the property should have a "set" method.
                    if (propertyInfo.CanRead) propertyRow["final"]="get{}";
                    if (propertyInfo.CanWrite) propertyRow["final"]=propertyRow["final"]+" set{}";

                            try { assemblyTable.Rows.Add(propertyRow); }
                            catch (System.Data.ConstraintException) {}

                    break;
                }
            }
        }
    }

    public static void printSource(DataTable assemblyTable)
    {
        string currentNameSpace="";
        string currentClass="";

        bool classOpened=true;
        bool firstInheritance=true;

        // -- First sort the table --
        DataRow[] rows=assemblyTable.Select("sortclass NOT LIKE '*+*' AND sortclass NOT LIKE '*<*' AND name NOT LIKE '*+*' AND type NOT LIKE '*+*'","sortclass ASC, line ASC");

        foreach (DataRow row in rows)
        {

            if (roseFlag)
            {
                System.Console.WriteLine();
                //System.Console.Write(row["sortclass"]);
                //System.Console.Write(" "+row["line"]);

                // Output a constructor as a method for Rose.
                if (row["metatype"].Equals("CO")) row["metatype"]="ME";

                System.Console.Write(row["metatype"]);
                System.Console.Write(" "+row["visibility"]);
                System.Console.Write(row["static"]);
                System.Console.Write(row["abstract"]);
                System.Console.Write(" "+row["name"]);

                if ( (""+row["type"]).Length>0) System.Console.Write(":"+row["type"]);
            }

            if (visioFlag)
            {
                string metatype=""+row["metatype"];
                string name=""+row["name"];

                if (metatype.Equals("CL") || metatype.Equals("IN"))
                {

                    if (!classOpened) System.Console.WriteLine("\n  {");
                    if (currentClass.Length>0) System.Console.WriteLine("  }");

                    classOpened=false;
                    firstInheritance=true;

                    currentClass=name;
                    string nameSpace="";

                    int lastDotPos=name.LastIndexOf(".");
                    if (lastDotPos>=0)
                    {
                        nameSpace=name.Substring(0,name.LastIndexOf("."));
                        name=name.Substring(name.LastIndexOf(".")+1,name.Length-name.LastIndexOf(".")-1);
                    }

                    if (nameSpace.Length>0 && !nameSpace.Equals(currentNameSpace))
```

```
                            {
                                if (currentNameSpace.Length>0) System.Console.WriteLine("}");
                                System.Console.WriteLine("namespace "+nameSpace+"\n{");

                                currentNameSpace=nameSpace;
                            }

                            if (row["visibility"].Equals("+")) System.Console.Write("   public ");
                            else if (row["visibility"].Equals("-")) System.Console.Write("   private ");
                            else  System.Console.Write("   ");

                            if (row["static"].Equals("$")) System.Console.Write("static ");
                            if (row["abstract"].Equals("@")) System.Console.Write("abstract ");

                            if (metatype.Equals("CL")) System.Console.Write("class "+name+" ");
                            else if (metatype.Equals("IN")) System.Console.Write("interface "+name+" ");

                            if (metatype.Equals("SC") || metatype.Equals("IM"))
                            {
                                if (firstInheritance && (""+row["name"]).Trim().Length>0) System.Console.Write(": ");
                                else if ((""+row["name"]).Trim().Length>0) System.Console.Write(", ");
                                System.Console.Write(""+row["name"]);
                                firstInheritance=false;
                            }

                            if (metatype.Equals("NC"))
                            {
                                if (!classOpened) System.Console.WriteLine("\n   {");
                                classOpened=true;

                                if (row["visibility"].Equals("+")) System.Console.Write("      public class");
                                if (row["visibility"].Equals("-")) System.Console.Write("      private class");
                                else  System.Console.Write("      class");

                                String nestedClassName=""+row["name"];
                                nestedClassName=Regex.Replace(nestedClassName,@"^.*\.",""); // Remove the package name
                                System.Console.WriteLine(" "+nestedClassName+" {}");
                            }

                            if (metatype.Equals("FI"))
                            {
                                if (!classOpened) System.Console.WriteLine("\n   {");
                                classOpened=true;

                                if (row["visibility"].Equals("+")) System.Console.Write("      public ");
                                else if (row["visibility"].Equals("-")) System.Console.Write("      private ");
                                else if (row["visibility"].Equals("#")) System.Console.Write("      private ");
                                else  System.Console.Write("      ");

                                if (row["static"].Equals("$")) System.Console.Write("static ");
                                if (row["abstract"].Equals("$")) System.Console.Write("abstract ");

                                System.Console.WriteLine(row["type"]+" "+row["name"]+";");
                            }

                            if (metatype.Equals("PR"))
                            {
                                if (!classOpened) System.Console.WriteLine("\n   {");
                                classOpened=true;

                                if (row["visibility"].Equals("+")) System.Console.Write("      public ");
                                else if (row["visibility"].Equals("-")) System.Console.Write("      private ");
                                else  System.Console.Write("      ");

                                if (row["static"].Equals("$")) System.Console.Write("static ");
                                if (row["abstract"].Equals("@")) System.Console.Write("abstract ");

                                // *** Remember that in this case the "final" flag contains the get{} set{} methods ***
                                System.Console.WriteLine(row["type"]+" "+row["name"]+" { "+row["final"]+" }");
                            }

                            if ( (metatype.Equals("ME")
                                && !(name.StartsWith("get_")||name.StartsWith("set_")))
                                || metatype.Equals("CO")
                               )
                            {
                                if (!classOpened) System.Console.WriteLine("\n   {");
                                classOpened=true;

                                //if (row["visibility"].Equals("+") || row["virtual"].Equals("v") || row["abstract"].Equals("@")) System.Console.Write("      public ");
                                if (row["visibility"].Equals("+") || row["abstract"].Equals("@"))
                                    System.Console.Write("      public ");
                                else if (row["visibility"].Equals("-")) System.Console.Write("      private ");
                                else if (row["visibility"].Equals("#")) System.Console.Write("      protected ");
                                else  System.Console.Write("      ");

                                if (!metatype.Equals("CO"))
```

```
                    {
                        if (row["final"].Equals("f") && row["virtual"].Equals("v"))
System.Console.Write("sealed ");
                        else if (row["final"].Equals("f")) System.Console.Write("final ");

                        if (row["virtual"].Equals("v") && !row["abstract"].Equals("@"))
System.Console.Write("virtual ");

                        if (row["static"].Equals("$")) System.Console.Write("static ");
                        if (row["abstract"].Equals("@")) System.Console.Write("abstract ");
                    }
//                      int openBracePos=name.IndexOf("(");
//                      string methodName=name.Substring(0,openBracePos);
//                      string parameters=name.Substring(openBracePos+1,name.Length-openBracePos-2);

                    String type=""+row["type"];
                    if (type.Equals("System.Void")) type="void";
                    if (metatype.Equals("CO")) type="";
                    System.Console.Write(type+" "+name);

//                      System.Console.Write(type+" "+methodName+"(");

                    //Regex paramRegex=new Regex(@"(^|,)\s*(?<paramType>[\w\.\s]+?)\s*(?=($|,))");
//                      Regex paramRegex=new
Regex(@"(^|,)\s*(?<paramType>[\w\.\s\]\[]+?)\s*(?=($|,))");
//                      Match paramMatch = paramRegex.Match(parameters);

//                      int pNum=0;

//                      for ( ; paramMatch.Success; paramMatch
//                                              = paramMatch.NextMatch())
//                      {
//                          if (pNum!=0) System.Console.Write(", ");
//                          System.Console.Write(paramMatch.Groups["paramType"]+" p"+pNum);
//                          pNum++;
//                      }

                    System.Console.WriteLine("{}");

                }

            }
        }

        if (!classOpened) System.Console.WriteLine("\n  {");
        if (visioFlag && currentClass.Length>0) System.Console.WriteLine("   }");
        if (visioFlag && currentNameSpace.Length>0) System.Console.WriteLine("}");

    }

  }
}
```

UML Software Design with Visual Studio 2010

Appendix B – Visual Modeling Web Site

I have created a supporting visual modeling web site where you will find the RE.NET Reverse Engineering source code and other resources.

Do drop in to see me at www.lotontech.com/uml.

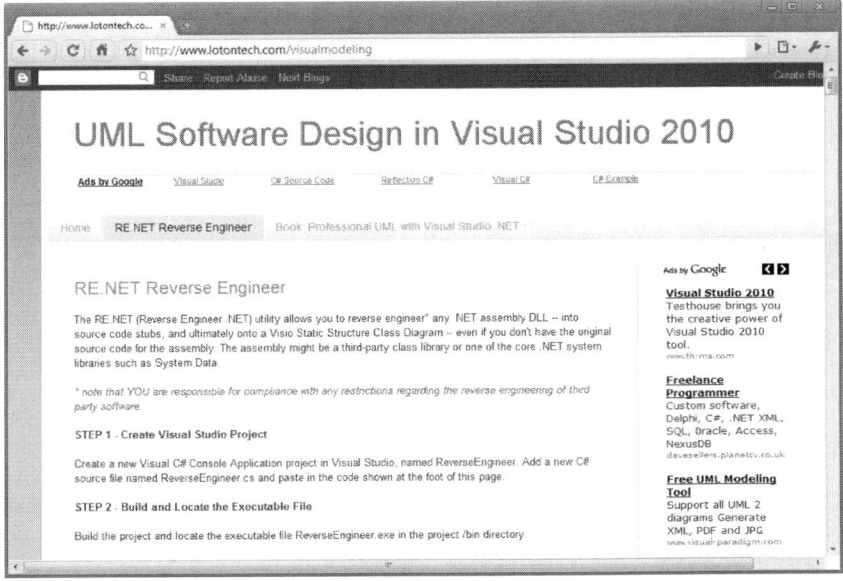

UML Software Design with Visual Studio 2010

Glossary of Acronyms

Due to its technical nature, this book is peppered with acronyms. While each one should have been spelled out on first usage, and periodically thereafter, you will no doubt benefit from the handy glossary that follows.

DGQL – Directed Graph Query Language

DLL – Dynamic Linked Library

DSL – Domain Specific Language

EXE – EXEcutable file

HTML – Hypertext Markup Language

IDE – Integrated Development Environment

MDA – Model Driven Architecture

MSF – Microsoft Solutions Framework

OMG – Object Management Group

RAD – Rapid Application Development

RUP – Rational Unified Process

TFS – Team Foundation Server

UML – Unified Modeling Language

VBA – Visual Basic for Applications

XDE – (Rational) eXtended Development Environment

XML – eXtensible Markup Language

UML Software Design with Visual Studio 2010

Also by Tony Loton

Tony Loton has previously co-authored the following related books for Wrox Press:

For the developer already familiar with UML and looking to get the best out of Visio, the Visual Studio .NET and Visio for Enterprise Architects combination is weakly documented, and the quality information needed to realize the time-saving features of Visio just does not seem to be available... until now.

In this book, you'll learn how to * Diagram business components in Visio * Generate code from a UML model * Reverse engineer Visual Studio .NET projects into a UML model * Reverse engineer into a UML model without source code * Document the project with UML and Visio * Design distributed applications with Visio's diagrams * Work with Entity Relationship database modeling, and round-trip engineering for database design.

A team of Microsoft insiders shows programmers how to use Visual Studio 2005 Team System, the new suite of products from Microsoft that can be used for software modeling, design, testing, and deployment.

Focuses on practical application of the tools on code samples, development scenarios, and automation scripting.

This timely book serves both as a step-by-step guide and as a reference for modeling, designing, and coordinating enterprise solutions at every level using Team System.

Code examples are provided in both VB.NET and C#

121

UML Software Design with Visual Studio 2010

Table of Figures

Figure 1 Positioning of This Book   12

Figure 2 End-to-End UML   20

Figure 3 Add a UML Diagram   28

Figure 4 Use Case Diagram Toolbox   31

Figure 5 Order Processing Use Case Diagram   33

Figure 6 Use Case Generic Dependency   34

Figure 7 Sequence Diagram Toolbox   36

Figure 8 Create Class for Lifeline   37

Figure 9 Rename Class in Properties Window   38

Figure 10 Add Message and Operation   39

Figure 11 Pick Stock Sequence Diagram   41

Figure 12 Interaction Use   42

Figure 13 Operation Signature in the Properties Window   44

Figure 14 Class Diagram Toolbox   46

Figure 15 Pick Stock Participating Classes #1   47

Figure 16 Specify Operation Visibility and Type   48

Figure 17 Add Association to Class Diagram   49

Figure 18 Pick Stock Participating Classes   50

Figure 19 Activity Diagram Toolbox   53

Figure 20 Example Activity Diagram — 55

Figure 21 Object Instance on Activity Diagram — 56

Figure 22 Order State-Chart Diagram — 57

Figure 23 Component Diagram Toolbox — 59

Figure 24 Example Component Diagram — 60

Figure 25 Partial Class Diagram — 64

Figure 26 UML Profiles — 66

Figure 27 Class Package Structure — 68

Figure 28 Add Visual C# Windows Forms Application — 76

Figure 29 Add Class Designer Class Diagram — 77

Figure 30 Class Designer Toolbox — 78

Figure 31 Pick Stock Participating Classes in Class Designer — 79

Figure 32 One-to-Many Association in Class Designer — 80

Figure 33 Generate Sequence Diagram, Step 1 — 83

Figure 34 Generate Sequence Diagram, Step 2 — 84

Figure 35 Less Detailed Sequence Diagram — 85

Figure 36 More Detailed Sequence Diagram — 86

Figure 37 Layer Diagram Toolbox — 87

Figure 38 Order Processing Layer Diagram — 88

Figure 39 Validate Architecture — 89

Figure 40 Class Dependencies Directed Graph Document   91

Figure 41 Analyzers / Unreferenced Nodes   92

Figure 42 Architecture Explorer   93

Figure 43 DGQL 'Public Classes' Query   94

Figure 44 Visio UML, Reverse Engineer   101

Figure 45 Reverse Engineered Code Classes in Visio   102

Figure 46 Reverse Engineered Code Visual Studio Solution   104

Index

.NET, 9, 11, 12, 13, 14, 19, 23, 70, 81, 83, 85, 99, 100, 103, 104, 107, 108, 121

Action, 51, 52, 54, 55

Activity Diagram, 18, 19, 51, 53, 55, 56, 61, 72

Activity Final Node, 51, 54

Activity Parameter Node, 52

Actor, 29, 31

Aggregation, 45, 50

Agile, 15, 71, 72

Analysis Model, 65, 68

architecture, 19, 69, 70, 88, 89

assembly, 19, 58, 103, 107, 108

Association, 30, 45, 48, 49, 79, 80

Booch, 14, 17

C#, 65, 75, 76, 77, 79, 81, 96, 103, 104, 107, 108, 121

Class Designer, 9, 24, 25, 75, 76, 77, 78, 79, 80, 95, 96

Class Diagram, 18, 19, 44, 45, 46, 49, 51, 75, 76, 77, 90, 107

code generation, 25, 96

Component, 19, 58, 59, 60, 67, 91

Component Diagram, 19, 58, 59, 61, 91

Composition, 45

Conceptual Design, 69

Decision Node, 51, 54

Delegation, 58

Dependency, 30, 33, 34, 45, 49, 58, 60, 86, 87, 89, 90

Design Model, 68

design pattern, 37, 89

Directed Graph Document, 69, 70, 75, 90, 91

Domain Specific Language (DSL), 13, 17, 24, 25, 78, 95, 119

façade, 91

field, 81

Fork Node, 51, 54

Generalization, 30, 59, 60

Implementation Model, 65, 68

Inheritance, 45, 47

Initial Node, 51, 53

Input Pin, 52, 54

Interaction Use, 36, 40, 41, 42

Interface, 45, 47, 59, 60

Jacobson, 14, 17

Join Node, 51

Layer, 61, 69, 75, 86, 87, 88, 91

Layer Diagram, 61, 69, 75, 86, 87, 88, 91

Lifeline, 35, 37, 44

Logical Design, 69

Merge Node, 51

method, 15, 36, 81, 83, 84, 113, 114

Microsoft, 9, 12, 13, 15, 17, 18, 23, 24, 25, 34, 66, 70, 72, 96, 121

Microsoft Developer Network (MSDN), 9, 95

Microsoft Solutions Framework (MSF), 9, 13, 15, 69, 70, 71, 72

Model Driven Architecture (MDA), 24

Model Explorer, 28, 35, 37, 38, 43, 44, 46, 65, 67, 72, 73, 87, 102

namespace, 50, 108, 115

Object Management Group (OMG), 18, 25, 96

Object Node, 51, 56

Object Oriented Software Engineering (OOSE), 17

one-to-many, 79, 80

Output Pin, 52, 54

Package, 45, 47, 67, 68

Part Assembly, 59

process, 15, 18, 19, 24, 51, 53, 57, 62, 63, 69, 70, 71, 72, 77, 96, 101, 102

profile, 65, 66

property, ii, 35, 79, 80, 81, 90, 114

Rapid Application Development (RAD), 15

Rational Rose, 23, 82

Rational Unified Process (RUP), 9, 72

reverse engineering, 83, 84, 86, 96, 101, 102, 103, 104, 107

round trip engineering, 76

Rumbaugh, 14, 17

Sequence Diagram, 18, 19, 35, 36, 37, 41, 44, 51, 81, 83, 84, 85, 86

State-Chart Diagrams, 56, 61

stereotype, 34, 65

subsystem, 32, 60, 65

swim lanes, 56, 62

Team Foundation Server, 15, 70, 72, 73

Team System, 9, 14, 24, 61, 72, 121

Test Case, 72

Unified Modeling Language (UML), i, 9, 11, 12, 13, 14, 15, 16, 17, 18, 20, 23, 24, 25, 27, 28, 29, 31, 34, 35, 37, 38, 43, 44, 46, 47, 49, 51, 56, 58,

60, 61, 62, 63, 65, 66, 67, 68, 69, 70, 71, 72, 73, 75, 76, 77, 78, 80, 81, 82, 83, 86, 87, 90, 91, 95, 96, 97, 99, 100, 101, 102, 103, 104, 108, 121

Use Case, 18, 19, 20, 29, 31, 33, 34, 40, 51, 53, 54, 60, 67, 72

Use Case Diagram, 18, 19, 20, 29, 31, 33, 51

User Story, 72

validation, 89, 90

version control, 73

Visio, 11, 12, 23, 24, 25, 27, 75, 82, 96, 99, 100, 101, 102, 103, 107, 108, 121

Visual Basic, 76, 81, 82, 86

Visual Basic for Applications (VBA), 82, 119

Visual Studio 2010, i, 11, 12, 13, 18, 24, 25, 27, 28, 49, 57, 61, 62, 69, 70, 75, 76, 82, 83, 86, 95, 96, 97, 99, 100, 101, 104

Visualization and Modeling Feature Pack, 25, 95

work item, 72

XML Metadata Interchange (XMI), 96, 97

The End

This is the last printed page of the book. If additional blank pages have been added by the printer, rest assured that you have not missed anything, and you can use the additional pages to make your own notes.

LOTON *tech*

www.lotontech.com

Printed in Great Britain
by Amazon.co.uk, Ltd.,
Marston Gate.